PIZZA CAMP

ABRAMS
NEW YORK

JOE
BEDDIA

PHOTOGRAPHY BY
RANDY HARRIS

RECIPES
FROM
PIZZERIA
BEDDIA

FOREWORD 13

INTRODUCTION 15

PART ONE:
BASIC PIZZA 20

EQUIPMENT 24

DOUGH 27

SAUCE 33

CHEESE 39

MAKE AND BAKE 41

THE GRAND FINALE 53

PART TWO:
WHITE PIZZA 58

WHITE PIZZA 61

ROASTED MUSHROOM CREAM 62

RICOTTA CREAM

SPRING CREAM

ROASTED OR FRESH GARLIC CREAM 64

CALABRIAN CHILE CREAM

ENGLISH PEA PURÉE 65

PART THREE:
TOPPINGS 68

SAUSAGE 70

SALAMES 74

BACON 77

ANCHOVIES 78

PROSCIUTTO, MORTADELLA, AND STEAK 80

MUSHROOMS 84

ONIONS 85

PICKLED CHILES 88

LONG HOTS 90

RANDOM WILD THINGS 91

GREENS 94

TRUFFLES 95

ROASTED PEPPERS 98

ROASTED FENNEL 99

PART FOUR:
COMPOSED PIZZA

ARRABBIATA PIZZA
109

ROASTED CORN, HEIRLOOM CHERRY TOMATO, BASIL PIZZA
112

BINTJE POTATO, CREAM, AND ROSEMARY PIZZA
115

ROASTED MUSHROOM PIZZA
116

DINOSAUR KALE, PICKLED RED ONION, AND SPRING CREAM PIZZA
121

SPECK, COLLARD GREENS, FONTINA, AND CREAM PIZZA
124

104

DANDELION GREENS, CALABRIAN CHILE CREAM, AND ROASTED RED PEPPER PIZZA 127

RAINBOW CHARD AND ROASTED GARLIC CREAM PIZZA 130

BROCCOLI, CHARRED ONION CREAM, AND CHILE PIZZA 133

SPINACH, RICOTTA CREAM, AND GARLIC PIZZA 134

DI FARA PIZZA 137

CREMINI MUSHROOM AND PEPPERONI PIZZA 140

PISTACHIO PESTO PIZZA 141

MARINARA AND ANCHOVY PIZZA 143

SICILIAN ALMOND PESTO PIZZA 146

MORTADELLA, RICOTTA CREAM, ROASTED PEPPER PIZZA 148

BREAKFAST PIZZA: SAUSAGE, EGGS, SPINACH, AND CREAM 151

ASPARAGUS, SPRING CREAM, ONION, LEMON PIZZA 154

PINEAPPLE, BACON, AND JALAPEÑO PIZZA 156

ZUCCHINI, CREAM, BASIL, AND GARLIC PIZZA 161

ROASTED FENNEL AND SAUSAGE PIZZA 162

STROMBOLI 167

PAN PIZZA 168

PART FIVE:
HOAGIES, SANDWICHES, ETC.

170

ITALIAN HOAGIE
177

VEGGIE HOAGIE
179

MEATBALL HOAGIE
183

PORK SANDWICH
185

OXTAIL HOAGIE
187

PEPPER + EGG
BREAKFAST HOAGIE
191

SMOKED SALMON
HOAGIE 193

CHEESESTEAK
195

HEIRLOOM
TOMATO HOAGIE
197

SMOKED SARDINE
HOAGIE 199

TOMATO BREAD
200

SAUSAGE BREAD
201

CROUTONS 204

BREADCRUMBS 205

I WAS JUST INVITED TO THE
JAMES BEARD HOUSE,
TO WASH THE DISHES.

gle Deck
1

overall.

eep.

overall.

eep.
cm)

overall.

eep.

cluding
exterior
a 1-1/4" x
Plus

nstant
izzas!
s on the
food

14P-1
Shown with standard S/S
front and 31" (78.7 cm)
gusset-style black legs.

FOREWORD

by Andrew Knowlton

In 2003, *Daredevil*, a movie starring Ben Affleck and Jennifer Garner, was released. It involved a blind martial-arts superhero. It was watched exclusively by people on airplanes. To coincide with the premiere, Howard Stern, one of Joe's heroes (it's true; I have no idea why exactly), held a contest. Stern asked serious fans to send him ideas for daredevil stunts that they would be willing to perform on his TV show. Next thing Joe knows, he's in a limo on his way to New York City to tape a segment. Let's just say that Joe's sketch involved a blindfold, a razor, shaving cream, and no pants. Joe did not win the $10K and a trip to the Playboy Mansion. Some guy who got shot in the ass with a paint gun did.

That story really has nothing to do with the book you're holding in your hands other than to embarrass Joe and point out that it wasn't the craziest thing Joe Beddia has ever done in his life. Not even close. No, that honor goes to his decision to open a pizzeria. Not just any pizzeria, but a 300-square-foot one with no chairs, no phone, no slices, no delivery, two employees, and only forty pies sold a day. You wouldn't let your worst enemy make such a dreadful decision, now would you?

But Joe Beddia is a pizza savant. In the four years since opening his shop, he has made every pizza that has come out of the oven at Pizzeria Beddia. And if Joe is sick or at a wedding or did too many drugs at, say, a Phish show and can't possibly make pizza the next day, then Pizzeria Beddia will be closed (that's only happened once).

Joe seemed to know his destiny even when I first met him back in 2008 when he was pouring beer at the South Philadelphia Tap Room. I was working on a story on Philadelphia's growing food scene, and Joe turned out to be the perfect informant. He knew which places cleaned their beer taps and which didn't. He knew what chef was an up-and-coming talent and who was tired. But his real nugget of intel was when he told me that he wanted to open up a pizzeria one day. I remember thinking, *Good luck, Joe*. I figured that was the last I'd see of that guy. I did mention him in my story, though, as the "affable bartender Joe Beddia."

Seven years later, in the July 2015 issue of *Bon Appétit*, I declared that the little pizzeria at 115 East Girard Avenue in the Fishtown neighborhood of Philadelphia made "The Best Pizza in America." Joe Beddia had kept his word and then some. Not only did that affable bartender end up opening his own pizzeria but it turned out to be one that people would wait four hours to try.

And now, here you are holding a book that *that guy* wrote. When Joe told me that he was going to do a cookbook that would show people how to make his pizza at home, I thought, once again, *Good luck, Joe*. But you know what? I should have known better. One day, Pizzeria Beddia will close (sorry to bum everyone out), and when you walk by the window, Joe won't be standing there making dough in his Phillies cap and his flour-covered apron. "There lived a pizza master . . . There lived a Pizza Jesus," people will say.

That's why I am once again grateful that I was wrong, and that Joe actually wrote this book. We'll always have *Pizza Camp* and with it a pizza master's manifesto.

If you do ever make it to Pizzeria Beddia, which I still think makes the best pizza in all of America, ask Joe about that *Howard Stern* episode. He won't get mad. Hey, at least he'll know you bought his book.

The New Short Course in Wine

FERGUS
HENDERSON

THE WHOLE BEAST

C·L·A·S·S·I·C SOURDOU

AST

WHAT HAPPENED TO ME?

Simple Ita

BEE

VETRI

MASTER

INTRODUCTION

"So how did you get into pizza?"

I always hate this question. Mainly because it's a really long answer—there are a ton of things that led me to pizza. Plus, I always assume that nobody really wants to hear my shit story anyway, but here it is. It's too loaded to distill it down to one or two reasons—I arrived where I am from a thousand places and ideas.

Everything starts when you're a kid. You taste your first things. Those tastes affect you, and you remember them for the rest of your life. I also think that as a cook, the early years are where you first draw from for inspiration. My mom's best friend's mother, who lived in downtown Lancaster after emigrating from Calabria and didn't speak much English, baked really crusty Italian bread once a week, and we'd eat that bread all week. Sometimes I would mow her tiny backyard with a push mower, and her husband would pay me a nickel. After I finished mowing, she would fry up peppers in olive oil and make me a simple sandwich. That was it: fried peppers and homemade bread. But I couldn't forget the flavor if I tried—it's still one of my favorite flavors. It seems like it's in my DNA.

For family Sunday dinners at my grandparents' house in nearby York, I can remember following my cousin Nunzio into the kitchen and ripping hunks of fresh bread and sneaking dips of the sauce that had been simmering for hours. It was loaded with meatballs and cuts of beef and pork—basically whatever was on sale that week.

I think that happy early childhood memories return throughout your life and become themes. Another big food memory: waiting for my dad to get home from work with a large cheese pizza from Argento's, my uncle John's pizzeria. It was perfect. Really nice dough with full flavor, fresh tomato sauce with a little oregano, and whole-milk mozzarella. Even as a kid I knew the difference between his pizza and the Pizza Huts and Domino's Pizzas of the world. Granted I still ate all the homogenized bullshit and pasteurized food of America. I liked Kraft macaroni and cheese as much as the next kid. But I was fortunate to have a family "just off the boat" from Sicily, so I knew what real food was. Like most immigrants, my family didn't have a lot of money, but we had tradition, and part of that tradition was making food from scratch. There weren't processed foods to be had. If it was your birthday, they would bake the cake.

Then my mother passed away and everything went black.

I went through elementary school, slowly going downhill. By the time I entered middle school, I had discovered "self-medication." I failed seventh grade. By the time high school arrived, I was stoned or tripping through a lot of it. Wah. Don't cry for me, Joe Beddia.

I made it out okay though. I'm still here, aren't I? Luckily I ended up at a satellite campus of Penn State in Reading for college. For some reason I decided to get into hotel, restaurant, and institutional management. The reason for this decision isn't clear to me, but I guess it sounded interesting. I mean at eighteen years old, what the hell do you really know about anything, much less what you want to do with the rest of your life? I was definitely interested in beer, which is kind of that industry. I brewed my first beer at eighteen. I probably tasted fifty world-class beers before I was twenty. I even kept a bottle collection in my apartment.

So I was going to school and working part-time at a Ralph Lauren outlet store—give me a break, I was nineteen—and I heard about a great bar in town that only served beer—hundreds of great beers, no crap—called the Northeast Taproom. Pete, the owner, was the bartender—it was practically a one-man operation. Well, Pete and his dog, Tapper. (The Taproom's still open, but Pete now runs Mike's Tavern, next to the Reading Phillies' stadium.) It was kind of a counterculture gathering place and an influential atmosphere. I would walk in dressed in a long-sleeve button-down with slacks and a tie, seeming at least twenty-one years old, and I looked around and realized I didn't want to work for the man, but for myself. Pete had such a simple, humble life, and I knew it was the life for me.

I stuck it out at Penn State for a couple of years, and at the end of the summer of '97, before I was to transfer to the main campus, I landed a job at Stoudt's Brewery, Pennsylvania's first microbrewery. I thought it would be a novel idea to brew beer for a living, and it was an exciting exit from formal education. I ended up having a long career in brewing that literally took me around the world. It was my first real career, and by the time I was finished with beer, I had worked at six breweries across three continents.

By 2004 I was working at a rather large brewery, and it began to feel like regular old factory work. I may as well have been making buttons or cars. I was just following recipes and making large batches, nothing creative. It was time for a change.

I reinvented myself as a twenty-eight-year-old busboy (hey, I went to school for hotel, restaurant, and institutional management, didn't I?). I found myself living in a changing and exciting time in Philadelphia. There was an opening at a new restaurant from Marc Vetri called Tria that concentrated on fermentation, which was right where I wanted to be—I was eager to learn more about the food industry. As I learned about wine while enjoying my new-found restaurant lifestyle, I started to get into pizza. There's no one real reason why I got into it. It was just that once I started exploring the best pizzerias, I wanted to learn how to make it. While getting ready for work, I would watch the daytime cooking shows on PBS. I remember one show in particular, where an East Coast chef visited pizzerias all over America and stopped in Phoenix to visit Pizzeria Bianco. I'm not sure why this spoke to me, except that Chris Bianco seemed to be an honest dude who had defied the odds: He was making some of America's best pizza in a desert, not in New York City, the capital of pizza. As a brewer, I knew the challenges of using your local brew-ing water when trying to replicate beers from around the world, and I knew it could be done even with beer's complicated alchemy. So it made sense that the myth "it's the water" could be worked with to make great pizza in challeng-ing locations. (Later I would discover that place isn't all that important: Tradition coupled with drive and great ingredients are paramount.)

In addition to my time at Tria, I also worked on Wednesdays, my day off, at Osteria as a *stagiaire* (a fancy French way of saying you are an unpaid trainee in a restaurant) in 2007. I was watching, helping, and learning on the pizza station at the wood-fired oven. And I decided to cold-call Chris Bianco to see what advice he could give for a career in pizza. What I didn't know is that one of the line cooks

at Osteria had arranged to work at Pizzeria Bianco for the summer. He didn't appreciate that I had reached out to Chris—I think he thought I was trying to compete with him. One morning while changing in the locker room before my shift, he came in and said, "Pack up your shit. Pizza camp's over."

That was my last day at Osteria.

In my spare time I was also making a lot of pizza at home, thanks to Peter Reinhart's *American Pie*. And if I wasn't making pizza at home, I was venturing into Manhattan and Brooklyn to visit historical pizzerias. It was my new hobby—I'd do some research, ask around, then travel just to eat at a new place. It got to the point where I'd go to three pizzerias in a day. I went to all the classics in New York, like Totonno's, Spumoni Gardens, and Una Pizza Napoletana. I really loved Una Pizza in the East Village (which has since moved to San Francisco)—Anthony Mangieri's dough is still the best I've had in America.

But the best day was when I discovered Di Fara Pizza. Domenico DeMarco opened this spot in 1964. He has made every single pizza at Di Fara since day one. He paid so much attention to detail: two mozzarella cheeses, chunky San Marzano tomato sauce, baked well and finished with a ton of extra-virgin olive oil, freshly grated cheese, and a bunch of freshly snipped basil. They looked amazing. It was a life-changing experience. No BS. I remember sitting down at one of the folding tables at the dingy pizza shop and tasting my first slice. I can remember laughing and almost crying at the same time. It was remarkable. The legend was true. It was the richest, most delicious American pizza, fully realized. It changed the way I look at pizza.

Then one day, while watching PBS, I caught a *NOVA* special about Japanese sword making. I was enamored with the swordmaker's dedication to the craft, and it made me think about those who'd made Hitachino Nest XH beer, a strong dark ale matured in *shochu* barrels that I'd recently tried and thought was delicious. So I called my phone company to find out how much a call to Japan would cost. It wasn't that much, so I hung up and cold-called Hitachino and spoke to the head brewer. After a series of emails with the owner of the brewery, we agreed that I would go to the Kiuchi Brewery (where Hitachino Nest is brewed), just north of Tokyo, and work there (as it turned out, I'd work Monday through Saturday, twelve- to fourteen-hour days) and get room and board in return. I wanted to leave after the first week, but my return ticket wasn't until five months later.

I never could have predicted how much I would walk away with after those months in Japan—not only would I have the best pizza of my life (the marinara from Savoy in Tokyo. It didn't even have cheese on it. It was like sorcery. Again with the laughter and tears), I'd figure out what I would do with my life. While it took me another five years to get my shit together, I knew that I wanted to open a tiny pizza shop essentially by myself.

After I returned to the States, I went to live with my brother Scotty in Madison. There, I worked for Derek Lee, the owner of Pizza Brutta, learning how to make fresh mozzarella and dough while feeding wood into the Neapolitan-style oven. I visited Chris Bianco's Pizzeria Bianco and Great Lake pizzeria in Chicago, and I toured pizza places in Italy, including stops at the Pizzarium in Rome and L'Antica Pizzeria Da Michele in Naples (you know, where Julia Roberts eats pizza in *Eat, Pray, Love*).

After a few months I moved back to Philly and worked in other restaurants, including a two-year stint at Zavino, running the pizza station. All the while planning to open my own pizza place.

What the line cook at Osteria didn't know at the time was that Pizza Camp had just begun. All my experiences and inspiration eventually led to the opening of Pizzeria Beddia on March 20, 2013. Those experiences, inspiration, and knowledge are also the foundation of this book. And not long after we opened, the guy who fired me came into the pizza shop and gave me a bottle of champagne.

PART ONE: BASIC PIZZA

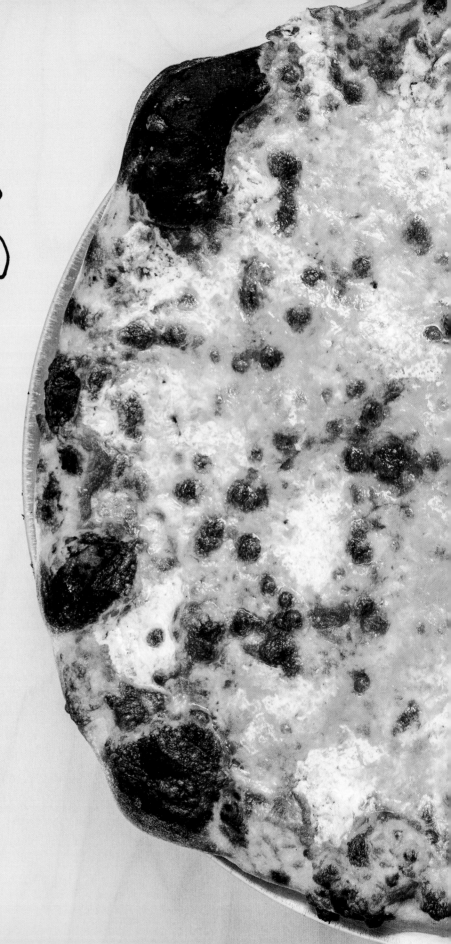

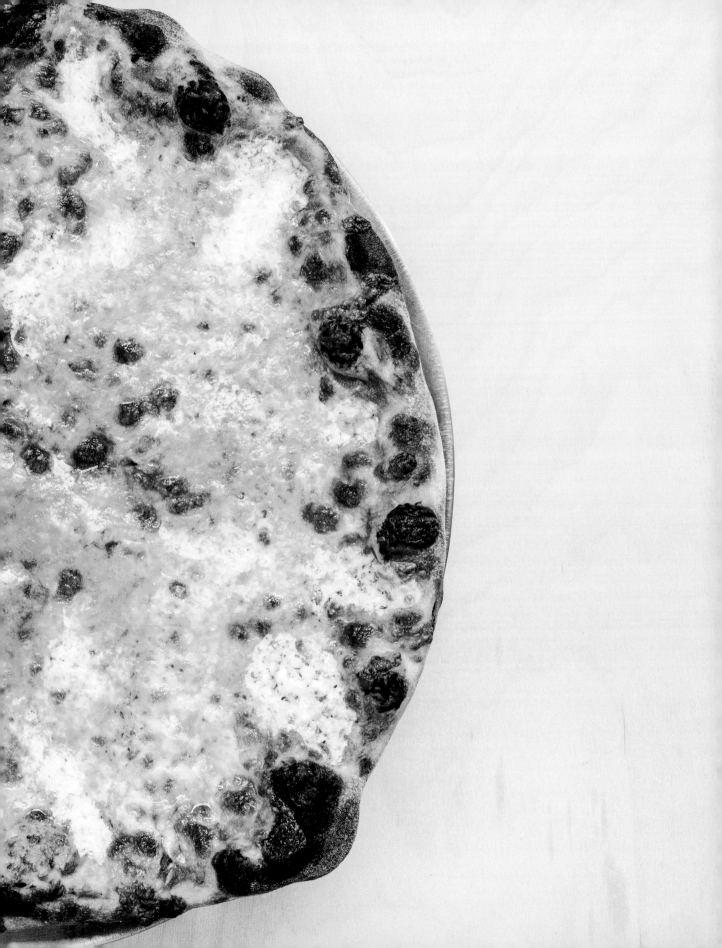

I feel like I came to pizza by being observant. By being a genuine fan. By seeing, tasting, and feeling. It was a culmination of life (or pizza) experiences. That's how I arrived at Pizzeria Beddia. All the pizzas that inspired me brought me right here: the Arizona olive oil that Chris Bianco finishes his pies with, Dom DeMarco's use of both fresh and aged mozzarellas, and the simplicity of Anthony Mangieri's Neapolitan pies.

Early in my pizza quest I was obsessed with the traditional, wood-fired pizzas of Naples. Using 00 flour, baking at 1,000°F (something like 540°C), making sauce with only San Marzano tomatoes from the volcanic soil of Mount Vesuvius—I felt this was the pure way forward. There are guidelines and rules to making these pizzas, and I wanted to follow them. But I slowly realized that all of my pizza heroes didn't really follow any strict codes. They created their own paths.

Before long, wood-fired pizzerias were en vogue and started popping up everywhere. Most of it is crap. To be honest, pizza is a quick food with great profit margins, but unfortunately people don't take the time to do it well. They're just interested in making a buck. Luckily, it took me a while to get my shit together and open the pizza shop. I spent a lot of time doing research and decided that I needed to do my own thing and separate myself from the competition. I had an inspired pizza on a trip with my brother to Chicago. It was at a tiny, now-closed pizzeria called Great Lake. They made a beautiful pizza in a slightly modified deck oven. I decided after that trip to stick with traditional American pizza—what some people would call New York–style. Lower baking temperature produces a crispier, more substantial crust than the wood-fired Neapolitan style, which tends to be softer and chewier.

Pizzeria Beddia is about quality. It makes your job easier as a cook when you start with great products. There is a lot of quality food close to the pizza shop and throughout the rest of the country. You no longer have to go to Europe for superior foodstuffs. We use organic flour from Utah, sweet New Jersey tomatoes, whole-milk mozzarella from Jersey, grassy California extra-virgin olive oil, and an aged raw cow's-milk cheese from nearby in Pennsylvania. I rely on all these ingredients to make great pizza. It is the humble marriage of a few cheeses, a solid tomato sauce, and a well-fermented crust.

When I was first opening Pizzeria Beddia, I knew I wanted to have an extremely simple menu. I've never liked big, complicated menus at places; nobody wants to be forced to make all those choices just to eat. I love the idea of "Here's what I have—get what you want." I'm not a pizza supremist.

That's why I've decided to organize this book the same way. The first two parts provide everything you need to know about making the staples at home—my #1 simple red pizza and seasonal white pizzas. Toppings can then be added to any or all of the pizzas you make, with some other ways to use dough (sandwiches, bread, etc.).

This book has recipes, but it's not a straight cookbook. Most cookbooks are stupid. I have a collection but they're mainly books I've been given (or borrowed—if you recognize one in the previous pages, you'll have to come get it yourself).

Fact is, I've spent my career figuring out the best way to make pizza and it's all in here, but you'll also have to put up with all my bullshit if you want it. The drawings, the bad jokes, the random notes and thoughts—if you want good pizza, you'll deal. I promise you it's worth it, just like the wait at my shop.

EQUIP- MENT

FOOD PROCESSOR

For blending cream sauces and making pesto.

PIZZA STONE

Get the largest pizza stone that will fit into your oven—one that will allow you to make a 16-inch (40.5-cm) pizza, ideally.

STAINLESS STEEL MIXING BOWLS

Get multiple sizes. I use these to mix my dough and for various *mise en place* needs.

DIGITAL SCALE

Essential for weighing flour, yeast, and other ingredients to make consistent dough. I weigh in metric. It's how I learned, and it's more precise than standard kitchen measurements.

PIZZA CUTTER

It's better than a knife!

CHEESE GRATER

You need it for hard cheeses. A good, sturdy metal box grater will work.

GARLIC PRESS

This is a very non-Italian thing to use, but I think it's great for distributing garlic into sauces and sausage. It's just easy.

PIZZA PEEL

This is the paddle you'll use to take your pizzas in and out of the oven. They come in both metal and wood; both types are fine. Just get one you feel comfortable using.

DOUGH CUTTER

Essential for portioning your dough. Google "dough cutter." You'll find a good one.

DOUGH SCRAPER

A pliable plastic tool, mainly used to move your dough from a bowl to the counter.

DOUGH

**Makes two 1-pound (454-gram) balls
(each makes a proper 16-inch / 40.5-cm pie)**

Important note while making dough: Turn your phone off and don't speak; it's a great time to listen, it's a great time for new ideas, it's not busy, you are present, and you are somewhere else. Making dough should be a calming, meditative process and a great time to think of new ideas about pizza, or about life in general.

1½ cups (355 g) cool water
2 teaspoons sugar
About ½ teaspoon active dry yeast
1 tablespoon extra-virgin olive oil
3½ cups (500 g) all-purpose or bread flour
1 tablespoon + ½ teaspoon fine sea salt

Pizza is bread. It's really simple and a little complicated at the same time. Dough takes planning to develop good flavor, and if you do it right you'll thank me later. You can make dough with a sourdough starter, but I've found that a nice, slow fermentation is more consistent and the results are always perfect. Sourdough can be unpredictable.

Find yourself a nice all-purpose or bread flour. I use organic flour, but regular King Arthur will do fine. Traditionally, four ingredients are used in making dough (flour, water, salt, and yeast), but we're adding sugar to help with fermentation and a little oil to relax and fatten the dough.

It took me a couple of years to come up with this process, which produces a dough with excellent flavor, a crispy exterior, and a chewy interior. These measurements are in metric, as traditional Italian recipes always are. This is how I initially learned how to do it. They are more exact, which is vital in baking.

Start out by whisking the water with the sugar and yeast in a large stainless-steel bowl. Next, mix in the olive oil. Then we'll mix in the flour. A large, strong spoon is good, or you can use your hands. If you have a stand mixer with a dough hook attachment, use that and mix for about five minutes on a slow speed, until everything is just incorporated. After everything is mixed and there aren't any dry parts, scrape any remaining dough down the sides and cover the bowl with plastic wrap or a damp kitchen towel. Let it rest for 30 minutes. This will give the gluten structure and strength. The dough will become elastic.

Next, knead the salt into the dough until the dough is smooth and the salt is fully incorporated, using wet hands (this makes handling it easier) or a dough scraper. Gently fold the dough over onto itself. You do not want to mix in the salt early on because it will hinder the yeast development. Once the salt is incorporated, cover the bowl with plastic wrap and put it in the fridge for 24 hours—the colder temperature will result in slower, longer fermentation, which in turn results in better flavor.

After the dough has chilled for 24 hours, take it out of the fridge and scrape it out onto a well-floured, clean counter. From here, you want to shape the entire thing into one big ball. With well-floured hands, grab either end of the dough mass and pull them up to meet in the middle. Rotate the dough mass one quarter turn and repeat. You're basically incorporating the dough into itself to form one smooth, round, floured ball. Flip the whole thing over, then, using a knife or bench scraper, cut the dough in half. You can weigh it to keep it even or eyeball it. I weigh everything to keep it kosher.

With well-floured hands, take one half of the dough and fold it over on itself, essentially repeating the same shaping technique with each half (see the pictures on pages 30 and 31), until you have a round, extremely smooth-surfaced ball. Consistency here is important, and it takes some practice to get it right, so don't get discouraged if it takes a few tries. If the dough gets too sticky or tacky while you're working it, dust it with more flour. After you have a smooth dough ball, set it on a floured surface and let it sit, covered with a kitchen towel, until it doubles in size. The climate, including temperature and humidity, plays a huge role in how fast this process happens. It should take approximately three to four hours. Just remember the goal is for it to double in size—that's when you know the dough is ready. It should feel smooth at this point, and it should rise back slowly when you press into it with your finger.

If you're not ready to make pizza right away, you can put the dough back in the fridge in a sealed container for another slow rise, but don't keep it in there for more than 24 hours, or it will begin to sour and become hard to work with.

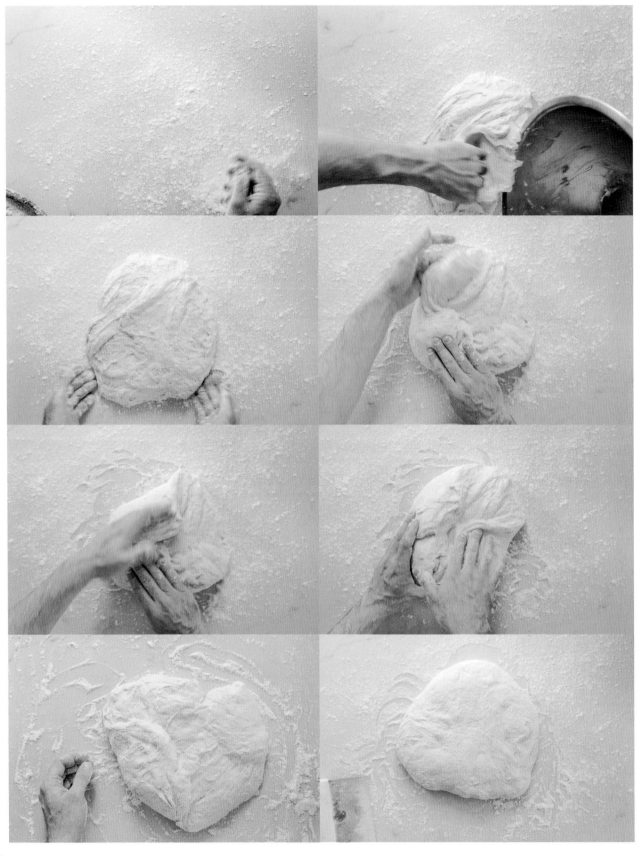

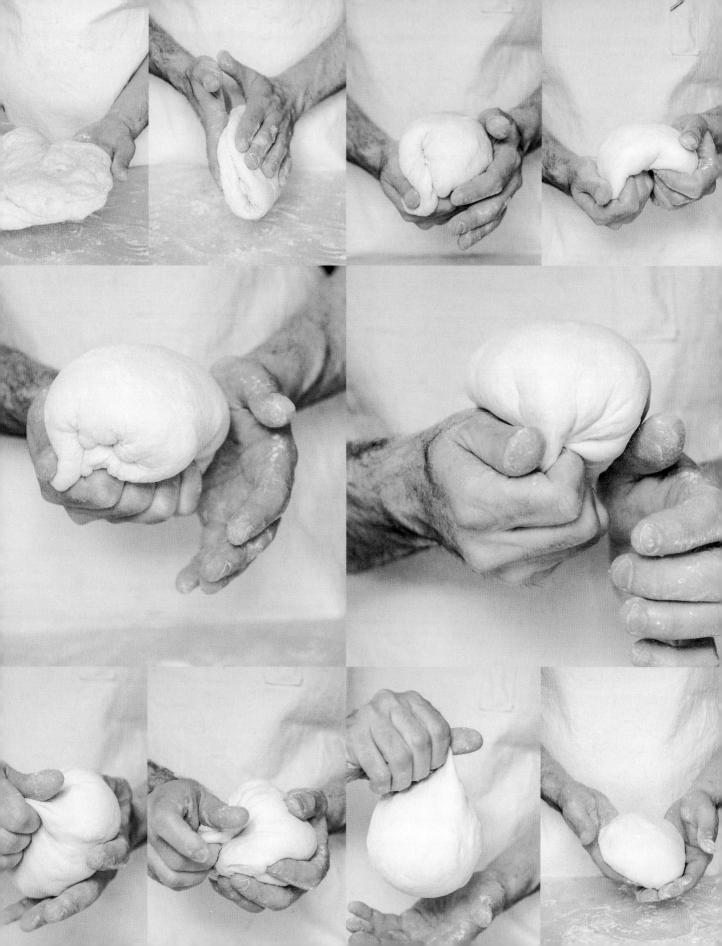

SAUCE

Makes 3½ cups (840 ml)

1 (28-ounce / 800-g) can crushed tomatoes or whole peeled tomatoes, crushed by hand or passed through a food mill
2 cloves garlic (don't buy the pre-peeled shit from China, for crying out loud!)
1½ teaspoons fine sea salt, or to taste
2 tablespoons extra-virgin olive oil

The dough is 95 percent of what you actually eat when you bite into a piece of pizza. So if you're like me and put a lot of time and love into the dough, you'll want a perfect sauce to complement all that hard work.

They never cook the sauce in Naples. This is the real secret. You don't want to use a concentrated ragu or pasty tomato sauce that will overpower everything. What you really want is a nice bright and clean tomato flavor that enhances your well-fermented dough and provides balance with your cheese-to-dough ratio.

Since you're really just marinating tomatoes, you need to start by finding the right tomato. This is one of the first Chris Bianco–isms that I committed to memory: "I can't tell you what the best tomatoes are. I know which ones I like, but as all our palates are different, you have to find your own." The right tomatoes aren't always the ones grown in the rich volcanic soil of Mount Vesuvius. The right tomatoes are the ones you like best. They should have a natural sweetness, a nice acidity, and a clean and bright tomato flavor. From here we do very little.

In Naples they traditionally crush San Marzano tomatoes by hand to make sauce. There are no seasonings or additions, only tomatoes. The sauce is spread on a round of dough and allowed to marry in a 1000°F / 540°C wood oven with fresh mozzarella, some olive oil, maybe a sprinkling of sea salt, and a few leaves of fresh basil or a sprinkling of dried oregano for aroma and taste.

I buy Jersey Fresh tomatoes. I like that they are local, have a natural sweetness, and come already crushed. You can buy whole peeled tomatoes and either pass them through a food mill (recommended) or crush them with your (clean) hands. (Don't use a blender. That introduces too much air into the tomatoes and makes them foamy.) And while I love the simple Neapolitan approach, I prefer to marinate the tomatoes with fresh garlic, extra-virgin olive oil, and sea salt ahead of time to let the flavors mingle.

Dump the crushed tomatoes into a nonreactive container, just large enough to store them in. Trim off any hard parts of the garlic; if there are green sprouts, leave them on. Push the garlic through a garlic press directly into the tomatoes. Add the salt and olive oil and mix thoroughly. You don't want the sauce to be too salty since it will cook and concentrate further on the pizza. Let it sit in the refrigerator for a few hours before using. You can store the sauce covered tightly in the refrigerator for up to one week.

CHEESE

At Di Fara in Brooklyn, Dom DeMarco uses a combination of both fresh and low-moisture mozzarellas, plus a hard cheese for finishing. Fresh mozzarella is best for a pizza that cooks quickly in a really hot oven, while shredded low-moisture mozzarella is suited for an American-style pizza that cooks at a lower temperature. At Pizzeria Beddia, we follow Dom's lead and use both mozzarellas to get that delicious buttery richness.

If you have a local cheese shop or specialty food store, shop there, at least for the fresh mozz, but grocery store cheese will be fine. Another key to choosing your mozzarella is making sure it is made with whole milk. If you're trying to cut calories, don't do it with your pizza.

Dom finishes his pies with Grana Padano, which is like a cousin of Parmigiano-Reggiano.

The goal of a finishing cheese is to add a rich, salty note right when the pizza comes out of the oven. If you add this cheese before baking, you will lose its nuanced flavor. At Pizzeria Beddia we use a locally made, cave-aged, raw cow's-milk gouda from Hidden Hills Dairy called Old Gold. Find a cheese that has been aged for more than a year and has a nice complexity. It will add another dimension while further seasoning and increasing the character of your already delicious pie. Parmigiano is great; a salty sheep's-milk Pecorino works well, too. If you have access to a good, local hard cheese that tastes great, then use that. Really, whatever hard cheese you personally think is the best cheese is what will work here. There's no right answer.

MAKE AND BAKE

Our goal is to replicate the brick oven we use at Pizzeria Beddia, which absorbs and radiates heat, for baking in your home. I recommend using a good baking stone. A thick stone will hold heat better and longer. If you don't already have a stone (or a baking steel), you can always go to a home supply store and buy a bunch of terra-cotta tiles. They come in all different sizes, so just get enough tiles to cover the rack of your oven. They're perfectly square so they fit together really well with no gaps—just find ones that fit your oven. Those work—trust me, I've tried everything. I have a large rectangular stone that fits perfectly on my home oven shelf. It's approximately 20 by 16 inches (50 by 40.5 cm) and about 1 inch (2.5 cm) thick. It's perfect; I bought it from The New York Bakers, which sells to anybody.

Place your stone on the lowest shelf of your oven, then turn your oven to its highest temperature. Most ovens go to 500°F (260°C) and some to 550°F (287°C). Heat your stone for at least one hour before baking.

Now that the oven is good, we can focus on the dough. If you're taking your dough out of the fridge, give it about 15 minutes or so to warm up a bit so it will be easier to work with. It should have doubled in size in the fridge. If it hasn't, let it sit at room temperature, covered with a slightly damp towel, until it does.

Next you can set up your "pizza station." Take the sauce out of the fridge. Then get your utensils ready: sauce ladle, dough scraper, and pizza cutter. You'll also need a medium to large bowl with a couple cups of flour in it. This will act as a dunk tank for your dough and for flouring your workspace. You'll also want a cup with a few ounces of semolina flour for dusting your pizza peel. Please do not use cornmeal. I find its texture distracting and don't think it belongs on a pizza.

Now you'll want to touch the dough to see if it's ready. When you press the dough with your finger, it should come back slowly. It should feel smooth and supple, like a butt cheek. If the dough doesn't feel ready, it needs more time out—keep an eye on it until it does what you want. (Just remember that leaving it out too long could cause it to over-proof.)

Lightly flour your counter and your hands. There is a lot of moisture in the dough, so you want to keep your counter and hands well-floured at all times—otherwise the dough will get sticky and impossible to handle. Lift the dough from its surface or container. If it doesn't seem to want to move, you'll have to use a dough scraper. Flip the dough into the flour bowl so the top side of the dough ball gets dusted first. Flip it once more, making sure that the dough is completely coated. Press the dough down into the flour, then pick it up and place it on the floured countertop.

Pressing your fingers firmly into the dough, start by flattening the center and work your way out toward the edge to make it wider, until it's about 7 to 9 inches (17 to 23 cm) wide. Pushing down on the dough will release some of the gas and actually begin opening up the dough. Be careful not to disturb the outermost lip. This will eventually become your crust.

The next step is a bit tricky. Your goal is to take this disc of dough and carefully stretch it to about 14 to 16 inches (35.5 to 40.5 cm) without tearing it or creating a hole. I pick it up with floured hands and begin to gently stretch it over my fists, letting gravity do most of the work.

Once you've stretched it enough, put the dough back on the counter, making sure there is a generous dusting of flour underneath. Take a few generous pinches of semolina flour and dust your pizza peel. Make sure it's coated evenly. Gently lift and transfer your dough to the peel. Make sure both your hands and the peel are well-floured. You are now ready to dress your pie.

Take approximately ¾ cup (180 ml) of sauce and spread it over the dough, all the way to the edges. Think of it like coloring as a kid—fill in the space without going over the lines. Your goal is to not get any sauce onto your peel.

Once the dough is evenly coated with sauce, add your fresh mozzarella. I normally use about 3 ounces (85 grams) for each pie. Take little clumps or pinches about the size of half a thumb and, starting on the outside and working your way in, place them evenly all over the pizza. But be careful not to crowd the middle—if you do, it gets too heavy and hard to transfer. Then add a medium to generous covering of shredded low-moisture mozzarella, about 2 cups (220 g).

This is a serious message (I'm warning you with peace and love): When dressing pizzas on the peel, do not, I repeat, do not leave your dough on the peel for an extended period of time. You should institute a five-minute-maximum rule. If you leave it on the peel for too long it will stick and not come off, forcing you to roll it up and make a stromboli-type thing. Which, in worst-case scenarios, is still pretty good. (See page 167 for a stromboli recipe.)

Now it's time to put the almost-pizza in the oven. With a firm and steady hand, take the peel and insert it into the oven at a slight downward angle, touching the tip of the peel to the back edge of the stone. This may not come easy on your first try, and it will take some practice to gain confidence. Give the peel a short jerk forward so that the dough begins to slide off the peel. Once you have the front end of the dough safely on the stone, gently pull the peel out and close the oven.

The hard part is over. It's time to let the oven do the work. Time your bake. It's best when your oven has a window and a light for watching the bake. I like to watch.

Let it go for 4 minutes. The crust will rise significantly. Then change the oven setting from bake to broil, cooking the pizza from the top down until the crust begins to blister. The residual heat of the stone will continue to cook the bottom. (If your broiler is at the bottom of your oven, skip this step and continue to bake the pizza as described.)

I cook all my pizzas until they're well done, which could take up to 10 minutes total (sometimes less). Just keep checking so you don't burn it. Look for the cheese to color and the crust to turn deep brown. It may blacken in spots, and that's okay.

When the pizza is finished baking, slide your peel underneath it in a quick motion so that the pizza is sitting directly on top of the peel. Take it out of the oven and place it on a cutting board. There it is: a glorious pizza.

NOTE: Do not use your peel as a cutting surface. I made that mistake early on and ruined the peel. A cutting board or an aluminum pizza tray is best.

THE GRAND FINALE

The addition of olive oil at the end adds flavor and richness. It also brings everything together. Traditional pizzerias in Naples finish their pizzas with cheap olive oil or grapeseed oil when they come out of the oven. Great American pizza makers like Chris Bianco use really nice oil. Chris uses a fruity extra-virgin oil made with Arizona olives. At Pizzeria Beddia we use a fruity, grassy extra-virgin oil made from Arbequina olives from California Olive Ranch. Just make sure you're using one that tastes great on its own. The best oils are buttery, fruity, and sometimes grassy. Drizzle the oil in a spiral from the outside in, about 2 tablespoons per pie.

Then grate your hard finishing cheese, like Parmigiano, over the pizza with a Microplane or the fine side of a box grater. Follow the same spiral pattern you did with the olive oil to cover the whole pie. I generally use 2 to 3 tablespoons of hard cheese per pie.

Finally, sprinkle a pinch of Sicilian oregano over the pizza, which will release a wonderful floral aroma. (Note that this step applies only to tomato-based pizzas.)

Now cut the pizza and eat it, too.

WHOA
WHOA
WHOA
STOP
THE
CLOCK

NATURAL WINE

What's natural wine, you ask? The most basic answer is that it's wine fermented with the natural yeast that lives on the skins of the grapes. Think of your grandfather or great-grandfather making wine with a lack of technology and a lack of pesticides. It's wine that changes from year to year, and it's generally a pure expression of the place it came from. Natural wine is a reflection of the winemaker's vision, but also of the soil and the specifics of the climate in which the grapes were grown. And guess what? It goes great with pizza.

The most popular types of wine are generally considered "new world"—modern styles from places like Australia, California, and South America. These are not usually my cup of tea. A lot of these wines are heavy with flavors of fruit and oak, and frankly lack the subtlety that I look for in wine. Honestly, the best quality of natural wine is that they are extremely versatile and pair far better with food than the new world stuff.

Luckily, natural wine producers are popping up in the new world places. I can remember opening my first bottle of Syrah from La Clarine Farm in the Sierra Foothills. I was so surprised by the flavors—light in body, spicy and funky like a good northern Rhône Syrah, but still clearly Californian. Broc Cellars out of Berkeley is another favorite. There is also great wine coming out of New York, from both the Finger Lakes and Long Island.

I wouldn't say that I'm some sort of expert, but I've come up with a simple way to find great wine. Here are two tips:

1. Find a good wine store, either one that has some sort of old head who looks like they've been in the wine game for a while, or a funky, hipster-type spot. There are stores like Chambers Street, Slope Cellars, and UVA in New York that will ship to you wherever you are.

They buy good wine in a variety of prices, mostly from smaller, family-owned vineyards. A good wine store usually won't buy mass-produced dumb wine.

2. Buy wine from a specific importer. There are hundreds—maybe even thousands—of importers, but a few stand out. Just like a good wine store that buys only good wine, you will find importers that make their living by creating great portfolios and bring in only quality products. I love David Bowler, Louis/Dressner, vom Boden, MFW, PortoVino, Zev Rovine, Jenny & François, and Selection Massale. I'm sure that I'm leaving out some good ones, but these are a great start.

Good table wine generally starts out in the low teens (one 750-ml bottle equals about five glasses). Wine gets a lot better in the $20 range. You get the point. I rarely spend more than $30 or $40 on a bottle. It depends on your budget and occasion, but you don't have to break the bank to drink well. And if you go out to a restaurant, I always recommend buying wine by the bottle. Even good restaurants usually don't have great wines by the glass. You'll get better wine and a better value if you buy the whole thing.

I pulled the bottles on the opposite page from my wine fridge, at random, and they're all great (I fucking hate wine snobs, but I know what tastes good). From left to right we have a wild Sicilian from high on Mount Etna (Frank Cornelissen), my favorite vineyard from the US of A (La Clarine Farm, this their Syrah), my favorite American producer (Broc Cellars, who makes a great Counoise), some dusty obscure Syrah from France (Gentaz-Dervieux), an excellent Pinot Noir from Germany (Enderle and Moll), some Riesling, which is my favorite lately (Jochen Beurer), and a wonderful, weird Prosecco (Ca' dei Zago).

It's important for me to note that just because a wine is a natural wine does not automatically mean it's good. There is stuff that goes too far out. It's like the annoying kid in school who tries too hard to be weird.

Cheers and happy hunting.

PART TWO:

WHITE PIZZA

Sometimes people come into the shop and ask me what I mean by fresh cream. I always say, "You know, like from a cow!" That's it. They usually get it after that.

I got the idea of adding fresh cream to a pizza from Nick Lessins at Great Lake pizzeria in Chicago. He basically said that the idea of a fresh cheese like mozzarella is that it tastes rich and creamy, so why not start with rich cream in the literal sense?

It's best to build a cream-based pizza with some texture first. So you'll add some cheese and greens or other veg—this will give the cream something to adhere to. That way, when you're sliding it into the oven, everything will remain on the pie. Infusing cream sauces with ingredients like garlic, roasted onions, or Calabrian chiles makes my job easier, and it also makes a better tasting pie by allowing the cream and ingredients to marinate ahead of time.

At Pizzeria Beddia we get a rich, fresh cream from a local farm. So if you have a good farmers' market or other specialty store, try their cream first. Regular heavy cream from the supermarket will work well, too.

I use 3 to 5 tablespoons of cream per pie—it all depends on how rich I want it.

White Pizza

Makes one 14- to 16-inch (35.5- to 40.5-cm) pizza

This is the most basic white pizza recipe. You can make it this way or sub any of the white sauces in the following pages or add whatever ingredients you feel like from the next section. I'm not trying to tell you how to live your life.

1 ball dough (page 27)
⅔ cup (165 ml) Spring Cream (page 64)
3 ounces (85 g) fresh mozzarella, pinched into small chunks
2 cups (220 g) shredded low-moisture mozzarella
Fine sea salt
3 tablespoons grated hard cheese
Extra-virgin olive oil

Preheat the oven and pizza stone to 500°F (260°C) or, if possible, 550°F (287°C). To make the pizza, first follow the instructions on prepping and rolling out the dough included in the Make & Bake section (page 41). Cover the dough with the Spring Cream, then add the mozzarellas. Season with salt. Bake as described in Make & Bake (page 41). Finish with the grated hard cheese and a drizzle of olive oil.

Roasted Mushroom Cream

Makes about 4 cups (960 ml)

I learned this recipe from Derek Lee at Pizza Brutta in Madison, Wisconsin. They roast button mushrooms in their wood-fired oven until they dry out a bit and their flavor intensifies. Then the mushrooms are puréed with raw red onion, cream, and rosemary. The resulting mix is amazing—both earthy and meaty.

At Pizzeria Beddia we top a pizza with this purée and thinly sliced sautéed cremini or oyster mushrooms. It goes on the menu in late winter, when fresh local produce is almost nonexistent, and it's a favorite of many of our regular customers.

2 (8-ounce / 225-g) containers button mushrooms (make sure they're clean, dudes —dust any dirt off with a paper towel)
3 tablespoons extra-virgin olive oil
Fine sea salt and freshly ground black pepper
2 sprigs of rosemary, finely chopped
1 medium red onion, roughly chopped
1 cup (240 ml) heavy cream

Preheat the oven to 450°F (230°C).

Toss the mushrooms with the olive oil, a couple of fat pinches of salt, and five turns on your pepper grinder. Spread them out on a baking sheet and roast for 20 to 30 minutes or until they lose their water and wrinkle a bit.

Place the mushrooms with their juices, rosemary, onion, and cream in a food processor or blender. Purée until there are no big chunks or pieces, but don't go too far or you'll have butter. It should be smooth and spreadable. Taste and adjust the seasonings as desired. This will keep in the refrigerator for about 5 days.

Ricotta Cream

Makes about 4 cups (960 ml)

I am not usually a fan of ricotta on pizza. It's often applied in thick clumps, which throws off the balance of every bite. I never like to have a whole mouthful of anything when it comes to pizza, regardless of what it is. This cream is a nice solution because it's really easy to work with and has the same rich flavor as straight ricotta. It's also a great base for sausage and fresh greens— those flavors just match up so well.

2 cups (480 ml) heavy cream
2 cups (480 ml) whole-milk ricotta cheese
Freshly ground black pepper
2 cloves of garlic, pressed or finely minced
Fine sea salt

In a large bowl, whisk the cream with the ricotta. I love lots of fresh pepper with this ricotta cream and usually add a couple tablespoons of freshly ground pepper. Lastly, add the garlic and season with salt. Mix to incorporate fully. It will keep in the refrigerator for about 5 days.

NOTE: Use a good fresh ricotta. I'd take sheep's milk over cow's milk, but it's harder to find. I would never use Sal's ricotta.

Spring Cream

Makes about 4 cups (960 ml)

This pizza marks the end of winter, when the only in-season ingredients have been mushrooms and potatoes for a few boring months. Winter in Philly is the longest season: It's cold, there's no parking, and everyone is angrier than usual. So when spring arrives and you emerge, like Punxsutawney Phil, from drinking in dark bars and see your fat, bloated shadow, this pizza—highlighted by a few fresh herbs plus lemon juice and zest for acid—will make you feel better about the world again.

1 handful of basil (10 to 20 leaves)
½ cup (25 g) chopped fresh fennel fronds
½ cup (25 g) chopped fresh chives
Zest and juice of 1 lemon
1 large clove garlic, pressed or minced
Fat pinch of red pepper flakes
4 cups (960 ml) heavy cream
Fine sea salt and freshly ground black
   pepper to taste

Combine all the ingredients in a food processor. Blend until slightly emulsified. It will keep in the refrigerator for about 5 days.

Roasted or Fresh Garlic Cream

Makes about 2 cups (480 ml)

This cream can go either way: Use roasted garlic for a sweeter, milder cream, and use chopped fresh garlic for a sharper, more vibrant garlic flavor. The roasted garlic goes really well with lighter toppings, and the fresh garlic cream will stand up better to meats and heartier greens.

1 or 2 heads garlic
1 to 2 tablespoons extra-virgin olive oil
2 cups (480 ml) heavy cream
Fine sea salt

For roasted garlic cream, preheat your oven or toaster oven to 400°F (205°C). Peel the garlic and place the cloves in a small foil pouch; drizzle with olive oil. Roast for about 40 minutes and you're done (the garlic should be really soft). Cut off any hard parts and combine with the heavy cream in a blender or food processor until slightly emulsified. Season to taste with salt.

For fresh garlic cream, peel one head of garlic. Chop or put the cloves through a garlic press (we use a garlic press as opposed to chopping it, but either works) and combine with the heavy cream in a food processor. Season with salt to taste and blend till emulsified. It will keep in the refrigerator for about 5 days.

NOTE: Don't be a dick and buy anything but fresh heads of garlic. Any sort of processed garlic sucks and has a weird acrid flavor. Don't do me like that!

Calabrian Chile Cream

Makes about 1 cup (240 ml)

Calabria is the "toe" of the Italian boot. In addition to preserved foods like 'nduja (spreadable salami) and cured varieties of sardines and cod (baccala), the region is famous for its chiles. The chiles, packed in oil, are lightly spicy, a little smoky, and kind of remind me of a salty cured olive.

I love to infuse their flavor into a cream using both the chile and the oil. It's spicy but not overwhelming, and it goes great with leafy greens (like kale or spinach) or heartier greens (like collards or Brussels sprouts). If you can't find jarred Calabrian chiles in your grocery store, you can order them online.

1 cup (240 ml) heavy cream
2 tablespoons chile oil from a
   jar of Calabrian chiles
6 to 8 jarred Calabrian chiles in oil, stems removed
2 cloves garlic, pressed or minced
Fine sea salt

Blend the cream, chile oil, chiles, and garlic in a food processor or blender until slightly emulsified. Taste and season with salt as desired. It will keep in refrigerator for about 5 days.

English Pea Purée

Makes about 2 cups (480 ml)

I love the pop and sweetness of a freshly shelled English pea. But they do start to ferment and get sour quickly if you don't use them—I learned that the hard way. Luckily frozen peas work really well here, too.

2 cups (290 g) shelled peas, fresh or frozen
1 clove garlic, pressed or minced
Handful of fresh mint leaves
Larger handful of fresh basil leaves
1 cup (240 ml) heavy cream
Fine sea salt and freshly ground
   black pepper to taste

Combine in the bowl of a food processor. Process until everything is incorporated but the mixture is still a little chunky. This purée goes really well on a pizza with pickled red onions (page 85) and fresh chives. It will keep in the refrigerator for about 5 days.

ART STUFF

This is an area that I don't pretend to know a whole lot about except for what I like. Philadelphia has a very rich collection of art and it is worth seeking out.

I'm a big fan of the sculpture here. Think Jacques Lipchitz, Jean Dubuffet, Roy Lichtenstein, Claes Oldenburg, Robert Indiana, Sol LeWitt, Isamu Noguchi, Mark di Suvero, and Auguste Rodin, to name a few. Not a lot of women on this list, which isn't my fault, but I'd love to see one of those giant spiders by Louise Bourgeois.

As I'm boasting, I'll also say that Mural Arts Philadelphia is the nation's largest public art program. So there.

Other places for art I love in Philly include the Barnes Foundation ($25 billion collection with master modernist and Impressionist paintings), the Pennsylvania Academy of the Fine Arts (a museum and art school started in 1805), the Rodin Museum (the largest collection from the sculptor outside of Paris), the Fabric Workshop and Museum (a museum that also has an artist residency program), and the Philadelphia Museum of Art (we have our own Cy Twombly and Marcel Duchamp rooms, along with more than 227,000 other works of art, like major Picassos and van Goghs).

My favorite place to visit just outside of town is the Wharton Esherick Studio. He was a painter turned sculptor / woodworker and one of America's first eccentric artists and craftsmen. You could drive up to New Hope and see famed woodworker George Nakashima's studio / compound, which is also amazing.

My editor says I should also mention the artists Keith Haring, David "Big Dutch" Nally, Jacques Lipchitz, Jean Dubuffet, Becky Suss, and Kent Twitchell, whose work I like enough to put in this book.

And lastly, go say hi to Claire at my favorite art gallery, Fleisher/Ollman. They have great contemporary art and cool outsider stuff, too. There is so much more, but I'm getting tired, so you'll have to take my word for it and come see for yourself.

PART THREE: TOPPINGS

SAUSAGE

Here are two sausage recipes—one from my uncle Pete and one we use at Pizzeria Beddia.

My uncle Pete swears by his sausage. It's the first I ever tasted. When I told him that I'd started making sausage, he asked, "Is there fennel in it?" Yes. "That's not sausage!" My aunt Donia and uncle Pete ran two lunch trucks together with my cousin John for more than twenty years. They made eighty pounds of sausage every week. He's a precise man with a good sense of humor—the type of guy you trust to handle raw pork. He'll coarse-grind pork shoulder and add salt and black pepper. That's it. There's a fair amount of black pepper, which gives it a little kick, but it's totally balanced and amazing because of its simplicity.

He always pinches a raw piece of the mix to taste if it's properly seasoned. That used to freak me out as a kid, but I started doing it myself. So, of course, when I made the sausage at Zavino in Philadelphia, I would do the same thing and freak out all the Mexican guys in the kitchen. Luckily you won't have to eat raw pork—you just have to follow the recipe. You can, however, tear off a little piece of the mixed sausage and fry it in a pan to taste it, and adjust the seasoning after.

The recipe we use at Pizzeria Beddia has fresh sage, garlic, a little fennel, and crushed red pepper. It has more going on than Uncle Pete's, but it's still subtle and well balanced.

We get our pork from a local farm in Lancaster. I recommend that you source yours locally, too. There is also your neighborhood butcher, or the grocery store meat department. The key is to get fresh meat that has nice fat on it, like pork shoulder. You don't want it to be too lean; lean is lame.

We grind our own sausage meat, so do the same if you have the equipment. Otherwise, have your butcher or meat department grind it fresh. Do not buy fine-ground packaged pork. Ask them for coarse-ground pork that will give you the nice meaty texture you really want.

Two pounds (910 g) of pork will yield more sausage than you need for making a couple pizzas, but that's the point. You can eat it for breakfast, make a sausage sandwich with fried peppers, or simply freeze it and use it the next time you make pizza.

Both recipes go well with the roasted onions (page 85) or any of the mushrooms in this section (page 84).

UNCLE PETE'S SAUSAGE

Makes 4 pounds (1.8 kg)

4 pounds (1.8 kg) pork shoulder or
  coarsely ground pork
2 tablespoons fine sea salt
2 teaspoons freshly ground black pepper

If you are grinding your own meat, cut the pork into 2-inch (5-cm) cubes. Coat the cubes with the salt and pepper, cover, and let sit in the fridge either overnight or for at least a few hours. Then take the cold pork—it grinds more easily and consistently right out of the fridge—and grind it using the coarse grinding plate. Pass the pork through twice—this will thoroughly mix everything.

CHUNKY SAUSAGE

If you are using fresh-ground pork from the butcher/grocery store, mix the salt and pepper in it the same day that they grind it. Ground pork doesn't have a great shelf life without salt. Make sure your pork is very cold when you mix it. After it's incorporated, cover it and put it back into the fridge. Now you have raw sausage.

The best way to use this on the pizza is by putting little pinches of raw sausage on your dressed pizza and letting them cook on the pizza in the oven. The 8 to 10 minutes that your pizza cooks will be plenty of time for the sausage. Plus, you'll end up with all the juices from the sausage directly on your pie. I love it this way. If you don't feel comfortable handling raw sausage, you can arrange the same pinches on a sheet tray and bake them in a preheated 450°F (230°C) oven for about 10 minutes. The sausage will be medium-rare—remember that it'll cook it again on the pizza, and you don't want to dry it out.

PIZZERIA BEDDIA'S SAUSAGE

Makes about 2 pounds (910 g)

4 teaspoons fine sea salt
2 teaspoons whole black peppercorns
2 teaspoons chopped fresh sage
2 teaspoons sugar
1 teaspoon crushed red pepper
1 teaspoon fennel seeds
1 medium clove garlic, peeled
2 teaspoons cold water
2 pounds (910 g) coarsely ground fresh
    pork shoulder, chilled

Put the salt, peppercorns, sage, sugar, crushed red pepper, and fennel seeds in a spice grinder and grind until incorporated. Place the spice mixture in a stainless-steel bowl large enough to comfortably mix the pork and seasonings.

Push the garlic through a press or Microplane directly into the bowl. Add the cold water to the spice mixture and stir to make a paste. Add the ground pork and mix until completely incorporated (this should take only a couple of minutes, so don't overmix it). Cover the bowl tightly with plastic wrap or transfer the sausage to an airtight container and refrigerate until needed. The sausage will keep in the refrigerator for up to 2 days.

The best way to cook this is to apply little pinches of raw sausage to your pizza dough, allowing it to finish on the pizza in the oven. Make sure to wash your hands before and after handling raw meat.

See above for cooking instructions.

SALAMES

This is the quintessential American pizza topping. For the first two years at Pizzeria Beddia, we served a great Calabrese-style salame (spicy and garlicky) from Olli in Virginia. It was perfect, but I felt a little bad for cooking such a beautiful cured thing on a pizza. Recently I discovered Salumeria Biellese in New York. They have a wonderful pepperoni that is the best I've ever had.

The thing is, I didn't want to serve people factory-farmed meat, or any other bullshit for that matter. For me, part of running a restaurant was serving only cured meat sourced from places I knew, where the practices used in raising that meat were responsible. I care about farms and farmers and knew my pizzas had to reflect that. One of my early thoughts in developing the pizzeria was *What would Willie Nelson do?* I don't know him, but I imagine he would always make the righteous choice. It's done me well to live by that code (when I remember it).

Hand-cut salame or pepperoni are what I put on my pizzas—I'd steer clear of pre-sliced grocery store stuff. Spread the slices evenly over the pizza. Less is more, especially when dealing with flavorful, fatty meats.

DUDE SEE IF YOU CAN SEE YOURSELF.

BACON

There are a few ways to bring bacon to a pizza. It goes well with my simple red sauce but can really be something special on a white pizza with a cream sauce. At Pizzeria Beddia we usually get a whole side of bacon and cut up lardons for even distribution. (A lardon is a small strip or cube of bacon, I'm told. I don't really speak French, but I know what they look like.) This allows you to have bite-size bursts of smoked porky flavor. I sauté these in a pan over low heat until firm but not crispy. You want to keep them medium rare so they finish cooking on the pizza, otherwise they'll be like beef jerky. If you really want to get crazy, you can reserve some of the fat and blend it with the cream. That's a little too heavy for me but still delicious.

Another way is to slow-cook strips of bacon in a pan on low heat until the fat starts to render out a bit and then you can arrange them on the pizza with a strip per slice.

Either way, I like to add some chives or another herb to cut through the richness and fat. Slices of jalapeño also work well on bacon pies.

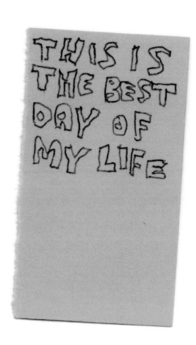

ANCHOVIES

I used to hate anchovies. I can remember as a kid, before I really appreciated them, my parents (assholes) would get a pizza with half anchovies (for them) and half plain (for us). The problem was that the pizza place would cook the hell out of the anchovies until they had an intense gross fishy flavor that permeated the whole pie.

It was all a matter of finding great anchovies and figuring out how to use them. The thing with anchovies, as with prosciutto, is that they go through an extensive curing process. This makes them beautiful—salty, of course, but also fruity and addictively savory. Even the average anchovy in the tin can is cured and requires no cooking.

This is the simplest of all toppings. The key is to find a great anchovy. The best are generally from the Mediterranean and packed in salt. These fish need to be filleted and rinsed before eating. Normally the same company that offers the whole anchovy in salt also has the same fish filleted and in oil. My favorite brand is Agostino Recca. These are the ones that we use at the pizza shop. The individual fillets are the same quality and a thousand times easier to cook with than the whole fish.

At Pizzeria Beddia we take anchovy fillets from Sicily and add them to the top of the pizza after it comes out of the oven. This allows them to melt a little, incorporate into the pie, and become aromatic. I usually try to break up one whole anchovy into two or three pieces over each slice—so about eight filets total per pizza. Just don't cook them!

PROSCIUTTO

The king of Italian ham. It even comes from Parma, the same place as the other Italian king, Parmigiano-Reggiano. It's aged from one to two years or even more. The resulting flavor is nutty, salty, almost sweet, rich, and buttery. You'd be a jerk to cook such a thing.

When it's fresh and sliced thin, it's perfect and needs little else. You'll want to dress your hot pizza when it comes out of the oven and then carefully arrange the prosciutto to cover the whole thing before you slice it. The fat will melt just so and will totally enhance your pizza. Feel free to add a little spicy arugula if you have any on hand.

You can actually find great prosciutto in America. A lot of good restaurants have solid charcuterie programs nowadays, and there is also La Quercia in Iowa, which does an excellent job. My favorite in Philadelphia is Joe Cicala's at Le Virtu. They use the best local pigs and do an amazing job.

MORTADELLA

The original bologna. Mortadella is cured pork that's spiced lightly and famous for its interspersed white cubes of fat. Sometimes it's made with black peppercorns and pistachios. I was a pretty picky eater as a kid and if something looked a little weird, like mortadella, I probably wouldn't eat it. But every time we would visit my aunt and uncle in northeast Philly, they'd serve it and we'd make sandwiches out of it, and that's when I fell in love with mortadella. Coming from Lancaster, my parents didn't really have access to it (we had Lebanon Bologna, which is a Pennsylvania Dutch thing).

Just like we do with prosciutto, we arrange thinly sliced mortadella over a hot pizza so the fat will melt a little. I would recommend putting the mortadella on a cream-based pizza over a red pie, as the flavors will be better suited and won't compete with the acidity from the tomatoes.

SPECK

The third in the trifecta in the family of approved (by me) Italian cured pork. Sometimes I like it even better than prosciutto because it's lightly smoked and still luscious. Speck also has a subtle spice from a cure of juniper, rosemary, and bay leaves. It's a thing of wonder.

Again, we arrange thinly sliced speck over a hot pizza so the fat will melt. I like to serve it like the mortadella, on a cream pizza, but it's strong enough to hold up to the acid of a tomato sauce, too.

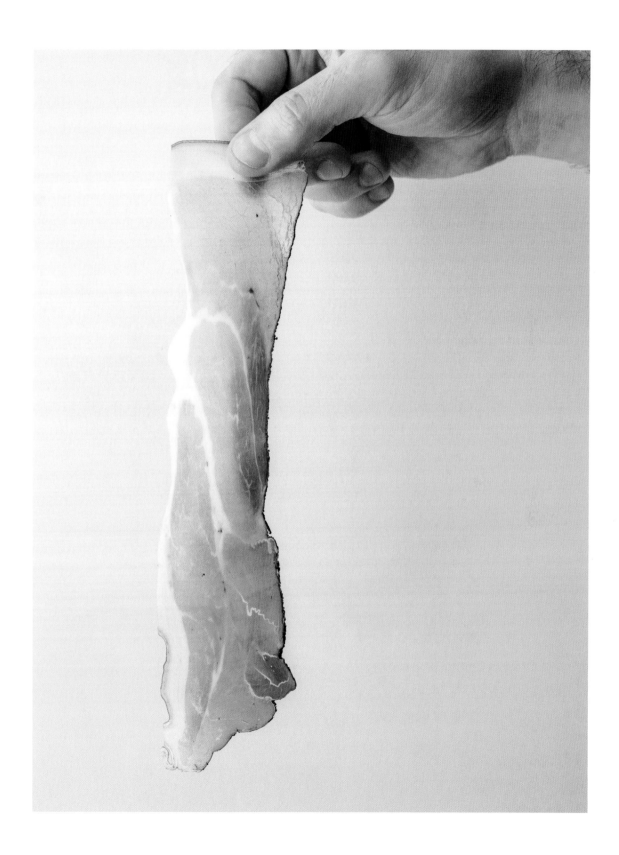

MUSHROOMS

A lot of people remark about the mushroom pie at Pizzeria Beddia, saying how amazing the mushrooms are. It's funny to me because we just slice raw cremini mushrooms and put them right on the pizza. Besides using fresh mushrooms, slicing them uniformly, and seasoning them, the oven does the rest.

The creminis in particular will sit on the mozzarella and incorporate into the sauce while the pizza bakes. The mushrooms will release moisture, but their liquid just adds more flavor to the pie.

My two other favorite mushrooms are shiitakes and oysters. They really benefit from a good pan-sear. Shiitakes are great because they lend an umami dimension that you'd normally get by adding meat or anchovies. And a crispy pan-fried oyster mushroom is actually close to meat in texture.

Mushrooms are easy to cook. You want to do them in batches. Don't overcrowd the pan, and make sure you use a neutral oil that can get really hot. Grapeseed and canola are good. Heat your pan over high heat, carefully add 2 to 3 tablespoons of oil, and then add your sliced mushrooms just when the oil starts to smoke. Let them cook for a couple of minutes before you start shaking the pan. This will give the mushrooms a chance to get a good sear—but it only happens if you leave them alone for a bit.

After 2 or 3 minutes, a crust should form; they're ready to flip/toss. I realize that part of the fun of cooking is constantly fucking around, moving and flipping shit, but that's never as good as cooking something to perfection, like a crispy oyster mushroom. Season liberally with salt after.

ONIONS

Raw

If you like a slightly sharper and less sweet onion flavor, thinly slice or shave red onions. These will have a much more assertive onion flavor than if you roast them, and they will end up cooking well while your pizza is in the oven for 10 minutes or so. Raw onion is great with sausage and cured meats.

Roasted

Take a nice sweet Vidalia or Spanish onion and roast the hell out of it: Slice the onion in half-inch (12-mm) strips, and toss them with extra-virgin olive oil, lots of fresh black pepper, and salt. Put them on a sheet tray and roast at 450°F (230°C) for 30 to 45 minutes. I don't stir them until the tips start to color or blacken a bit. They'll come out soft with some crispy edges and a deep sweet onion flavor, and they will match perfectly with sausage or mushrooms.

Quick Pickling

Makes 1½ to 2 cups (240 to 360 ml)

Pickling red onions tempers their natural sharpness and introduces a little additional sweet character. They end up being a really simple pairing with a cream-based pizza, since the acid cuts through the sauce well.

½ cup (120 ml) red wine vinegar
¼ cup (60 ml) white wine vinegar
3 tablespoons fine sea salt
2 tablespoons sugar
1 teaspoon whole black peppercorns
1 bay leaf
1 clove garlic
2 medium red onions, sliced or shaved

Combine 1 cup (240 ml) water with both vinegars, salt, sugar, peppercorns, bay leaf, and garlic in a small saucepan over high heat. Bring the mixture to a boil, then strain out the solids and add the onion slices. Let the onions steep in the pickling liquid for 15 to 20 minutes. Drain and they're ready to use right away. You can also transfer them to an airtight container and store in the fridge for up to 2 weeks.

Chives & Scallions

The most laidback of all onion flavors (and my favorites) are chives and scallions. Just finish the pizza with finely chopped chives or scallions when taking the pizza out of the oven. They will add a freshness that will help lighten a cream pie.

PICKLED CHILES

Makes 1½ to 2 cups (240 to 360 ml)

We've served these chiles since day one at the pizza shop.

I've always been a huge fan of the half-sours that you get at a proper Jewish deli. They have that salty, garlicky crunch that every pickle should have. Honestly, half-sours are not soured at all, they are just pickled in a salt and garlic brine. They have an excellent texture and are a cinch to make.

Here, we apply the same principle to serrano chiles. They are one of the greatest complements to your pizza, especially if you like it a little spicy. And they add a great crunch, too.

3 cloves garlic, minced or crushed
2 tablespoons fine sea salt (the resulting brine should taste slightly less salty than seawater)
12 serrano or jalapeño chiles
1 teaspoon to 2 tablespoons crushed red pepper (optional)
2 cups (480 ml) hot water (the hottest you can get from your faucet)
2 glugs of white wine vinegar (optional)

The first thing I do is make the brine. Place the garlic in whatever nonreactive container you'll store the pickles in. A quart-size (960-ml) glass mason jar works best. Put the sea salt on the garlic. This is a good time to slice off the tip of one of the chiles crosswise and give it a taste. If it's not as hot as you like, go ahead and add some crushed red pepper flakes to the garlic and salt. If the chile blows you away, omit the red pepper flakes.

Add the hot water to the container with the garlic and salt, along with the vinegar (if using). Stir and set the brine aside to let the flavors marry while you slice the chiles.

Put some freaking gloves on and be careful not to touch yourself, especially down there. Thinly slice the chiles and add them to your brine. Cover the container and let the chiles pickle for 48 hours at room temperature. Once they're done pickling, you can use them immediately or store them in the fridge for up to 2 weeks.

LONG HOTS

You can add a long hot to anything or eat them on their own. They're the sort of thing you'll find in an Italian deli as a sandwich topping. They seem like a very Philadelphia thing to me, but I don't really know. You have to be careful with these things, as they are generally medium spicy but can be ridiculously sharp and super hot. There is no way to tell how hot they're going to be until you taste them.

Wash about a dozen long hot peppers. Add a few teaspoons of neutral oil to a large skillet and sauté the peppers over medium heat. I generally cover with a lid and let them soften—should take about 20 to 30 minutes. I keep the stems on until I eat them. Season with salt and let cool. Refrigerate. They are good for about a week, or you can freeze them.

MOUNT ETNA IS AN ACTIVE VOLCANO.

RANDOM WILD THINGS

There is a small window at the beginning of spring in Pennsylvania, as well as in other forest-and-meadow locations throughout the nation, where wild things pop up: ramps, green garlic, fiddleheads. Mostly stuff found by venturing into nature. Or if you're like me, stuck in the pizza shop all day, you can find a forager. Or seek them out at your local farmers' market. Wherever you find these wild things, trust me: They all belong on a pizza.

The one thing to remember with wild greens is that you need to be careful when washing them. A lot of times, wild greens are coming straight from the earth and can be dirty or a little sandy. The short period that these greens are available can really turn your pizza into spring magic.

Ramps and Green Garlic

Ramps are probably my favorite. If you're not familiar with them, think of a green onion with a couple of long green leaves extending from a bulb. They add a fresh, garlic-like flavor without the intense bite. I treat them the same way that I would a scallion—I thinly slice the bulbs and cook them right on the pizza, and use the garlicky stems like an herb to garnish. The same goes with green garlic, which is young garlic. These are easy spring finds at the farmers' market. They have a larger bulb with much longer green leafy stems than ramps. Again, we cook these bulbs right on the pizza and leave the green stems for garnish.

Fiddleheads

Fiddleheads have maybe the shortest season of all the wild things. They are like tight little curled fern sprouts. Usually you would blanch or sauté them before eating, but I just toss them in a little oil and cook them right on the pizza. They go really well with a cream-based sauce finished with ramps or green garlic. They have a unique, fresh, vegetal flavor that isn't really replicated anywhere else.

GREENS

At the shop, we do a lot of white pizzas, which work extremely well with greens. Think cream, garlic, spinach, and mozzarella. Whether it's broccoli rabe, brassica, spinach, rainbow chard, dinosaur kale, collard greens—it doesn't matter, they all taste great on a pizza.

We have great local farms, and a lot of the year we get beautiful fresh greens. We generally put them over a cream base at Pizzeria Beddia. They're a customer favorite at the shop. I think they go well on red pies, too, especially arugula and other microgreens, with a little extra garlic. I don't blanch or sauté any of them ahead of time—some we put on before the pie goes in the oven and some after it comes out.

Hearty

I like to put heartier greens—such as broccoli rabe, brassica something, spinach, rainbow chard, dinosaur kale, and collard greens—on the pizza before it goes in the oven. I love how some parts melt a bit and others develop a crispy texture. Just make sure that they're clean and seasoned with salt. The only thing to really be aware of is woody stems, which I usually cut out. I like to use the whole thing if I can. For instance, when we get kale I will pull off and finely chop the stems and add them to the pizza for a little texture. And you definitely want to keep the colorful stems of rainbow chard for their beauty. It all ends up cooking well and tasting great after 10 minutes in a hot oven.

Tender

Put more tender greens, like arugula, on a really hot pizza after it comes out of the oven and let them wilt a little before chowing down. You can dress the greens in a vinaigrette before topping the pizza, but at Pizzeria Beddia I add the greens dry and finish with a little extra-virgin olive oil. Mustard and microgreens, even your average mesclun mix, are great, too. You basically want to use greens that will wilt a bit and whose peppery flavor will freshen up your pizza experience, helping to balance the richness of the cheese.

TRUFFLES

Truffles and pizza are pretty amazing together. The intense flavor and aroma will bring your pizza party to an impressive place. I definitely use a cream-based sauce and keep it simple to ensure that the thousand-dollar-a-pound mushrooms remain the star of the show.

Think cream, some mozzarella, roasted onion, and some creminis. The cremini mushrooms will accentuate the flavor of the truffle. You could use some greens, too—just keep it simple.

I recommend trying to buy a truffle straight from a restaurant. If you have or could become friends with a local chef, they will be able to get truffles at a cheaper cost when they're in season. If money doesn't matter, you could go to one of the fancy gourmet stores. You'll really just need a small truffle for a pizza or two anyway.

Most of you, I'm assuming, won't have a truffle slicer. They're pretty cheap if you want one, but a Microplane works fine. It won't look as pretty, but you'll cover more surface area and the results are perfect. If you don't have a Microplane, then go get one. They're great not just for truffles but for citrus zest, cheese, garlic, ginger, etc.

ROASTED PEPPERS

One of my earliest food memories was eating a sandwich of homemade Italian bread and roasted green peppers. Even though I was only seven, the simplicity and humble nature really struck me. The experience has stayed with me, like a dream flavor I want to return to.

So now I like to honor that memory by constructing pizzas with that same idea of simplicity. You don't need five or six things to build flavor, just a few done well. Green bell peppers are not for everyone, as they can be slightly bitter, so feel free to use the sweeter red, orange, or yellow ones.

At the pizza shop, we don't have an open flame, so I just roast them in the oven. I like the way the flesh breaks down, but you don't get smoky nuance without an open flame. So if you have a grill or stovetop gas burner, use it. Using a pair of tongs, slowly turn the pepper over a medium flame until the pepper is entirely blackened, about 5 minutes. To slow roast them in the oven, take a couple washed peppers and place them on a sheet tray lightly coated with a neutral oil in a preheated 450°F (230°C) oven. Wait for the skin to char and blister. The peppers will be done once they deflate a bit, after about 10 minutes.

For both methods, immediately place the cooked hot peppers in a tightly covered bowl or sealed container. Let them sit for 20 to 30 minutes. Once the peppers have cooled enough to handle, peel and discard the skins, but save any accumulated juice. Cut the peppers, toss the seeds, and slice into ½-inch- (12-mm-) wide strips. Toss with the pepper juice, add a couple tablespoons of extra-virgin olive oil, and season with salt to taste. You can also marinate them with chopped garlic, basil, and a little crushed red pepper. Let them sit covered in the fridge for an hour before use.

ROASTED FENNEL

Makes 1 cup (150 g)

Like the roasted peppers, this is another simple and delicious pizza topping. We will make good use of the entire fennel plant, and since we're adding stuff to the fennel, here's the recipe.

1 bulb fennel
1 tablespoon whole fennel seeds
2 tablespoons extra-virgin olive oil
2 shots sambuca
Fine sea salt and freshly ground black pepper

Preheat the oven to 450°F (230°C).

Cut off all of the fennel's fronds (the hairy, dill-like extensions of the stalks). Separate the stalks from the bulb. Cut the bulb into quarters. Carefully and thinly slice both the stalks and the bulb on a mandoline. If you don't have one, try and slice the whole thing evenly and thinly with a sharp knife.

Crush a tablespoon of fennel seeds into a powder—a mortar and pestle or a spice grinder will do. In a large bowl, combine the crushed fennel seeds, the olive oil, the shots of sambuca, salt, and freshly ground pepper to taste, and the sliced fennel stalks and bulb. Transfer to a sheet pan and roast until the fennel is nicely colored, about 30 minutes. Chop the fennel fronds and add to the roasted fennel when finished. This is a great topping paired with other vegetables and a perfect complement to either of the sausages (page 70).

PART FOUR: COMPOSED PIZZA

Hey, maestro, conduct me a pizza.

These are pizzas I've put together over time at the pizza shop. Most have come together by accident. A lot of times the farmer dictates what we put on a pizza based on what's growing in his or her fields. We've had to adapt what we make to the rhythm of the seasons. We are forced to be creative based on what we're given. This has allowed me to grow as a cook and discover new vegetables, new flavors, and new combinations of flavors. I follow the simple rule of buying good products and letting them speak for themselves, and the pizzas always turn out delicious.

Since much of this came together as a result of luck, happenstance, or trial and error, I fully support you taking these guidelines and running with them. Please experiment with these recipes as freely as you'd like, even incorporating ingredients we talked about in the previous section.

ARRABBIATA PIZZA

Makes one 14- to 16-inch (35.5- to 40.5-cm) pizza

I can remember reading about Chris Bianco and his Rosa pizza. He basically said this pizza was a true expression and representation of who he was. I initially found the statement funny and a little pretentious—but Chris is a really humble dude. I knew that until I actually tasted the pizza, I wouldn't understand what he was talking about.

The Rosa pizza was brilliant. It was like tasting the terroir of Arizona (where his pizza shop is), the Bronx (where Chris is from), and Italy all at once. Then what he said made sense. It was proof that you can catch a glimpse of someone through their craft.

The Arrabbiata is my pizza. It's what I want to eat, but it's not for everyone. "Arrabbiata" means "angry" in Italian. What's angry about this pizza is its heat. Like me, it's bold and perhaps a little obnoxious. If you could describe a pizza as somewhat self-destructive, it is this one. On the positive side, it's immensely flavorful and equally addictive. Just like me, if you get to know me.

I've found when talking to customers that they will let you know what it's like to digest spicy food and experience its inevitable disgusting return. We know, we know. But my favorite quote is: "Put the toilet paper in the freezer tonight."

For the sauce:
Makes about 2 cups (480 ml)
1 cup (240 ml) grapeseed oil or other neutral oil
20 Thai chiles, stems removed, finely chopped
5 large cloves garlic, pressed or minced
1 (28-ounce / 800-g) can crushed tomatoes
Fine sea salt
10 large fresh basil leaves, torn

For the pizza:
1 ball dough (page 27)
3 ounces (85 g) fresh mozzarella, pinched into small chunks
2 cups (220 g) shredded low-moisture mozzarella
3 tablespoons grated hard cheese
Extra-virgin olive oil

Preheat the oven and pizza stone to 500°F (260°C) or, if possible, 550°F (287°C).

Heat the oil in a medium saucepan over medium heat. Add the chiles and garlic and sauté for a few minutes, then reduce the heat to low and simmer, uncovered, for 30 minutes.

Remove the pan from the heat and stir in the tomatoes. Season to taste with salt and stir in most of the basil, reserving some for garnish. This will keep in the refrigerator for about 5 days.

To make the pizza, first follow the instructions on prepping and rolling out the dough included in the Make & Bake section (page 41). Spread 2 cups (480 ml) of the arrabbiata sauce on the dough, going all the way to the edges, being careful not to go over. Bake as described in Make & Bake (page 41). Finish this pizza with the remaining torn basil leaves, the grated hard cheese, and a drizzle of olive oil.

ROASTED CORN, HEIRLOOM CHERRY TOMATO, BASIL PIZZA

Makes one 14- to 16-inch (35.5- to 40.5-cm) pizza

This is the number one customer favorite at the pizza shop. First off, we have great corn for about three to four months. It's really sweet, especially after you roast it. The summer heirlooms in Pennsylvania and New Jersey are renowned. The flavors are bright and sweet and all make sense.

½ pint cherry tomatoes

Fine sea salt and freshly ground black pepper

Fat pinch of crushed red pepper flakes

½ cup (120 ml) extra-virgin olive oil,
    plus more for drizzling

4 ears sweet corn

½ cup (120 ml) heavy cream

Handful fresh basil (10 to 15 leaves)

Zest and juice of ½ lemon

1 ball dough (page 27)

3 ounces (85 g) fresh mozzarella, pinched into
    small chunks

2 cups (220 g) shredded low-moisture mozzarella

3 tablespoons grated hard cheese

Preheat the oven and pizza stone to 500°F (260°C) or, if possible, 550°F (287°C).

For the tomatoes, slice them in half and place them in a medium bowl. Season with salt, pepper, the crushed red pepper, and a drizzle of olive oil. Let them marinate for at least 30 minutes at room temperature.

Shuck the corn. Be careful to remove all the hair or whatever that's called. Don't buy the pre-shucked stuff either. Do it right.

Place the shucked corn on a rimmed baking sheet and lightly coat the ears with olive oil and salt and pepper. Roast until the corn gets some color and caramelization. Not too dark, just good color. Let them cool.

Now for the tricky part. With a chef's knife, carefully cut the ears in half. Place the cut side down so the half ear is standing up. No lawsuits please. Starting at the top, shave the kernels off the cob, careful not to cut into the cob. After your corn is shaved, run the back of your knife down the same side to get the rest of the corn and its "milk" off the cob.

Take all your corn and it's "milk" and place it in the bowl of a food processor. Add the cream and season liberally with fresh pepper and salt to taste. Blend until you have a slightly chunky yet creamy consistency. You could also skip the food processor and just purée it in a large bowl with an immersion blender. This will be the sauce.

And lastly, the basil. I like to make a simple basil oil because it prolongs the life of the basil. Place the basil in a food processor or blender, along with the ½ cup (120 ml) of olive oil, the lemon zest and juice, and salt and pepper to taste.

To make the pizza, first follow the instructions on prepping and rolling out the dough included in the Make & Bake section (page 41). Spoon a liberal amount of roasted corn cream (about ⅔ to 1 cup / 165 to 240 ml) over your dough. Add your mozzarellas. Then evenly coat with marinated tomatoes. To bake, follow instructions in Make & Bake section (page 41). Finish with some basil oil and grated hard cheese. Also feel free to sprinkle some of the marinated tomato juice over the finished pie. Enjoy!

BINTJE POTATO, CREAM, AND ROSEMARY PIZZA

Makes one 14- to 16-inch (35.5- to 40.5-cm) pizza

I was turned on to potato pizza during my first trip to Rome. There was a little pizza shop there, which is now wildly famous, called Pizzarium. They were the best pizzas I ate in Italy, even though they are far from traditional.

For this recipe I use a bintje potato. I was introduced to the bintje by one of our farmers, Ian Brendle from Green Meadow Farm. It has a great earthy character and flavor. This is the potato most used in Belgium and France for their famous fries. If you can't find bintje, Russet potatoes will do fine.

You might feel the desire to add bacon or ham to this pizza, but I urge restraint. Let the humble potato be the star.

2 or 3 bintje potatoes, or 2 large
    Russet potatoes, approximately 1 pound (450 g)
Extra-virgin olive oil
Fine sea salt and freshly ground black pepper
1 ball dough (page 27)
3 ounces (85 g) fresh mozzarella,
    pinched into small chunks
2 cups (220 g) shredded low-moisture mozzarella
3 to 4 tablespoons heavy cream
1 sprig rosemary, finely chopped
2 tablespoons finely chopped chives
3 tablespoons grated hard cheese

Preheat the oven to 450°F (230°C). (Your pizza stone should be in the oven for this entire process.) Place the potatoes on a rimmed baking sheet, toss them with liberal amounts of olive oil, salt, and pepper, and bake for 1 hour or until tender when pierced with the tip of a knife. Remove them from the oven and let them sit at room temperature until they are cool enough to handle.

Increase the oven temperature to 500°F (260°C) or, if possible, 550°F (287°C). To make the pizza, first follow the instructions on prepping and rolling out the dough included in the Make & Bake section (page 41). Then take the whole potatoes and crumble them into rough one-inch pieces. Sprinkle these pieces evenly over the dough, leaving small, mashed piles with the skin and all.

After the potato is on, spoon the cream over the top in a circular motion. Add your mozzerellas. Season one last time with a sprinkling of sea salt. If you feel the need to add ham or bacon, now's your chance. I really think you should try it first without. Bake as described in Make & Bake (page 41).

After you're done baking, the potato should be a little crispy and browned. Next, we'll finish with the rosemary and chives, a drizzle of olive oil, and the grated hard cheese.

ROASTED MUSHROOM PIZZA

Makes one 14- to 16-inch (35.5- to 40.5-cm) pizza

This is the earthiest, richest, most savory pizza that I've ever tasted and another favorite at Pizzeria Beddia. It's inspired by a pizza that I learned to make at Pizza Brutta in Madison, Wisconsin. We serve it in late winter, when mushrooms are one of the only local products available. Start with the Roasted Mushroom Cream (page 62) and add pan-seared shiitakes and crispy oyster mushrooms. Thinly sliced raw creminis are an easy substitute here, too (they cook quickly, so no need to pre-sauté them). This pizza delivers a lot of depth that is both savory and meaty and ridiculously delicious.

1 ball dough (page 27)
⅔ cup (165 ml) Roasted
   Mushroom Cream (page 62)
3 ounces (85 g) fresh mozzarella,
   pinched into small chunks
2 cups (220 g) shredded low-moisture mozzarella
1 heaping cup (110 g) sautéed
   mushrooms (page 84)
2 tablespoons chopped fresh chives
3 tablespoons grated hard cheese
Extra-virgin olive oil

Preheat the oven and pizza stone to 500°F (260°C) or, if possible, 550°F (287°C). To make the pizza, first follow the instructions on prepping and rolling out the dough included in the Make & Bake section (page 41). Spread the roasted mushroom cream on the dough. Add your mozzarellas. Spread your sautéed mushrooms evenly around. Bake as described in Make & Bake (page 41). Finish the pie with the chives, grated hard cheese, and a drizzle of olive oil.

DINOSAUR KALE, PICKLED RED ONION, AND SPRING CREAM PIZZA

Makes one 14- to 16-inch (35.5- to 40.5-cm) pizza

It makes me laugh that people are impressed by pickling. You can pickle something in 30 minutes, no practice or prior knowledge necessary. The pickled element really balances out the flavor and richness with the acid.

1 ball dough (page 27)

⅔ cup (165 ml) Spring Cream (page 64)

3 ounces (85 g) fresh mozzarella, pinched into small chunks

2 cups (220 g) shredded low-moisture mozzarella

4 to 5 handfuls roughly chopped or torn dinosaur kale leaves, 4-inch (10-cm) pieces are fine

½ cup (55 g) pickled red onions (page 85)

3 tablespoons grated hard cheese

Extra-virgin olive oil

2 tablespoons chopped fresh chives

Preheat the oven and pizza stone to 500°F (260°C) or, if possible, 550°F (287°C). To make the pizza, first follow the instructions on prepping and rolling out the dough included in the Make & Bake section (page 41). Liberally coat your dough with the spring cream. Add your mozzarellas. Add the kale, then your cooled pickled onions. Bake as described in Make & Bake (page 41). Finish with the grated hard cheese, a drizzle of olive oil, and the chives.

IF YOU SEE ME IN YOUR RESTAURANT FOR "RESTAURANT WEEK"
IT'S JUST TO USE THE BATHROOM.

SPECK, COLLARD GREENS, FONTINA, AND CREAM PIZZA

Makes one 14- to 16-inch (35.5- to 40.5-cm) pizza

This is a hearty pizza where you take a cold cured pork and let it melt over a hot pie. It's reminiscent of my first visit to the famed Pizzarium in Rome. There they use bresaola, a cured beef. I substitute with speck because it is rich and smoky.

For this pizza, we'll go a little lighter on the mozzarellas because we're introducing another cheese. Fontina is a wonderful northern Italian cow's-milk cheese from the same area where the speck is produced.

1 ball dough (page 27)
⅓ cup (35 g) coarsely grated fontina cheese
3 ounces (85 g) fresh mozzarella, pinched into small chunks
2 cups (220 g) shredded low-moisture mozzarella
4 to 5 handfuls coarsely chopped collard greens
3 to 5 tablespoons heavy cream
Fine sea salt
3 tablespoons grated hard cheese
Extra-virgin olive oil
4 paper-thin slices of speck

Preheat the oven and pizza stone to 500°F (260°C) or, if possible, 550°F (287°C). To make the pizza, first follow the instructions on prepping and rolling out the dough included in the Make & Bake section (page 41). Sprinkle the dough with the fontina and both mozzarellas. Then come the collards. These will break down and marry with the cheeses. Drizzle on the cream and season with a little salt. Bake as described in Make & Bake (page 41). When the pizza is done, finish with the grated hard cheese and a drizzle of olive oil. Then arrange the speck over the whole pie and slice. This is a great pie with a cold glass of natural Riesling. Think Keller, Beurer, or J.B. Becker. Mama mia!

DANDELION GREENS, CALABRIAN CHILE CREAM, AND ROASTED RED PEPPER PIZZA

Makes one 14- to 16-inch (35.5- to 40.5-cm) pizza

Dandelion is a bitter green that grows wild in Sicily, where people are really good at making do with what they have. Find your fresh dandelion greens at a farmers' market. The bitterness of the greens will be tempered by the sweetness of the roasted peppers, the garlic-heavy cream, and the mild heat of the chiles.

1 ball dough (page 27)
3 heaping tablespoons Calabrian
   Chile Cream (page 65)
1 clove garlic, very thinly sliced
3 ounces (85 g) fresh mozzarella, pinched
   into small chunks
2 cups (220 g) shredded low-moisture mozzarella
½ cup (55 g) roasted red peppers
4 to 5 handfuls coarsely chopped dandelion greens
Fine sea salt
Extra-virgin olive oil
3 tablespoons grated hard cheese

Preheat the oven and pizza stone to 500°F (260°C) or, if possible, 550°F (287°C). To make the pizza, first follow the instructions on prepping and rolling out the dough included in the Make & Bake section (page 41). Spread the Calabrian chile cream on the dough. Add the garlic, then your mozzarellas, roasted red peppers, and finally the dandelion greens. Season with a pinch or two of salt. Bake as described in Make & Bake (page 41). Finish with a drizzle of olive oil and the grated hard cheese. Enjoy the old country.

I EAT PIZZA
AND I SLEEP
PIZZA BUT I
NEVER DRINK PIZZA.

RAINBOW CHARD AND ROASTED GARLIC CREAM PIZZA

Makes one 14- to 16-inch (35.5- to 40.5-cm) pizza

Rainbow chard is one of my favorite pizza greens because of its earthy, hearty flavor and bright colors. (Regular Swiss chard will do.) It cooks really well, doesn't get overpowered by garlic, and melts right into the dough. It's also stunning to take the big, beautiful leaves and drape them over a pie, the cheese accented by the red, pink, and orange stems.

1 ball dough (page 27)
⅔ cup (165 ml) Roasted Garlic Cream (page 64)
3 ounces (85 g) fresh mozzarella, pinched into small chunks
2 cups (220 g) shredded low-moisture mozzarella
4 to 5 handfuls coarsely chopped rainbow chard leaves
Fine sea salt
2 tablespoons finely chopped fresh chives (optional)
3 tablespoons grated hard cheese
Extra-virgin olive oil

Preheat the oven and pizza stone to 500°F (260°C) or, if possible, 550°F (287°C). To make the pizza, first follow the instructions on prepping and rolling out the dough included in the Make & Bake section (page 41). Spread the roasted garlic cream on your dough. Top with your mozzarellas, then carefully lay out the chard to cover the pie, leaving no uncovered space, even over the edges. Season with salt. Bake as described in Make & Bake (page 41). Finish with the finely chopped chives, if using, the grated hard cheese, and a drizzle of olive oil.

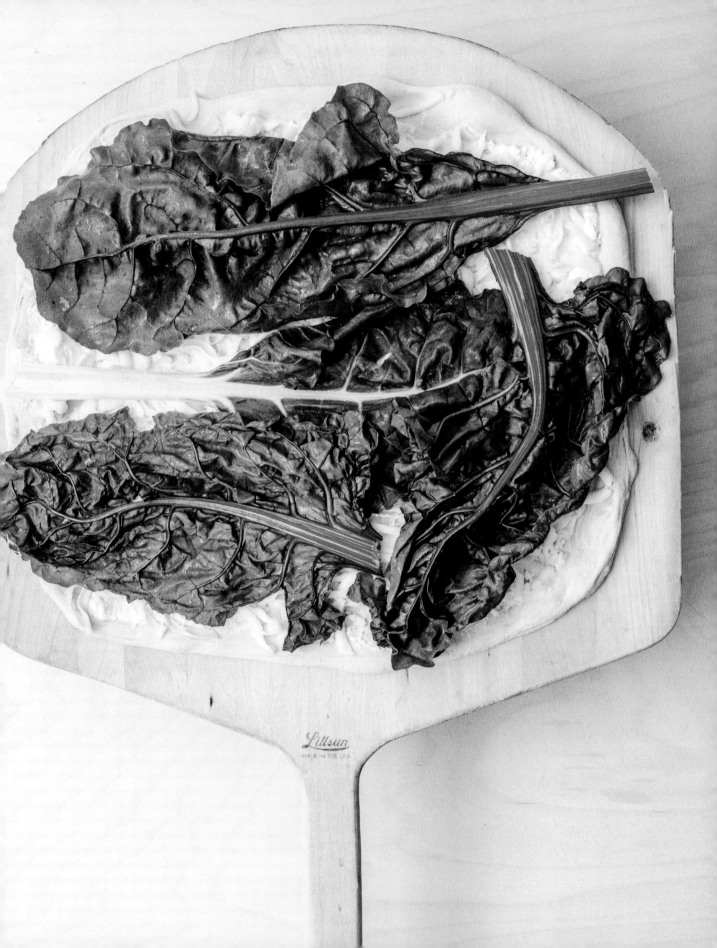

BROCCOLI, CHARRED ONION CREAM, AND CHILE PIZZA

Makes one 14- to 16-inch (35.5- to 40.5-cm) pizza

For the sauce:
Makes about 2 cups (480 ml)

1 large Vidalia or other sweet onion
Extra-virgin olive oil
Fine sea salt and freshly ground black pepper
1 cup (240 ml) heavy cream
3 to 7 Calabrian chiles packed in oil, stems removed
   (don't wuss out)

For the pizza:

1 ball dough (page 27)
3 ounces (85 g) fresh mozzarella, pinched into small
   chunks
2 cups (220 g) shredded low-moisture mozzarella
1 medium head of broccoli, broken down in ½-inch
   (12-mm) pieces, stems included!
3 tablespoons grated hard cheese

Preheat the oven and pizza stone to 450°F
(230°C).

Slice the onion into half-inch (12-mm) strips.
Toss the strips well with olive oil, salt, and
pepper, then spread them out on a rimmed

baking sheet and bake for about 20 minutes.
The ends of the onion slices should curl
up and start to color and blacken. Give them
a stir and continue baking for another
20 minutes. The onion should be browned
with some blackened edges. Remove the baking sheet from the oven and let it cool slightly,
then throw the onions in a food processor or
blender with the cream, salt and pepper to
taste, and the Calabrian chiles. Blend until
smooth. This will keep in the refrigerator for
about 5 days.

Increase the oven temperature to 500°F
(260°C) or, if possible, 550°F (287°C). To
make the pizza, first follow the instructions on
prepping and rolling out the dough included
in the Make & Bake section (page 41). Spread
about 3 heaping tablespoons of the sauce
on your dough, then top with the mozzarella
cheeses, the broccoli pieces, and a pinch of
salt. Bake as described in Make & Bake (page
41). Finish with the grated hard cheese and a
drizzle of olive oil.

SPINACH, RICOTTA CREAM, AND GARLIC PIZZA

Makes one 14- to 16-inch (35.5- to 40.5-cm) pizza

I feel like this is the first white pizza. Simple, old school, classic. Don't forget to sprinkle a little crushed red pepper on at the end. See if you can get good spinach, too. The washed baby spinach isn't the best regarding flavor. You really want the larger crinkly spinach in bunches with the roots on. You can never go wrong with simplicity, and this is a prime example.

1 ball dough (page 27)
⅔ to 1 cup (165 to 240 ml) Ricotta Cream (page 62)
3 ounces (85 g) fresh mozzarella,
    pinched into small chunks
2 cups (220 g) shredded low-moisture mozzarella
2 large cloves garlic, very thinly sliced
3 to 5 cups (60 to 100 g) baby spinach
Fine sea salt
3 tablespoons grated hard cheese
Extra-virgin olive oil
Crushed red pepper flakes

Preheat the oven and pizza stone to 500°F (260°C) or, if possible, 550°F (287°C). To make the pizza, first follow the instructions on prepping and rolling out the dough included in the Make & Bake section (page 41). Spread the Ricotta Cream on your dough, then add both mozzarellas. Distribute the garlic slices evenly. Top with what looks like too much spinach. Season with salt. Bake as described in Make & Bake (page 41). Finish with the grated hard cheese and a drizzle of olive oil. Sprinkle some crushed red pepper flakes on—as much as you think you can handle.

DI FARA PIZZA

Makes one 14- to 16-inch (35.5- to 40.5-cm) pizza

This is a tribute to one of the greatest pizzas I've ever eaten, made by the incomparable Dom DeMarco. I remember tasting it for the first time at his small Brooklyn shop, and laughing really hard because it was so good, so rich, so creamy, with great tomato flavor and lots and lots of basil. It's the single best slice of American pizza I've eaten—nothing else has come close.

His sauce is chunkier than mine, and if you really want to replicate it you'll take a can of whole tomatoes and break them up with your hands, leaving some larger pieces or strips of tomatoes, and season to taste with salt. About a full cup of the sauce per pie will do.

1 ball dough (page 27)
1 cup (240 ml) tomato sauce (page 33)
3 ounces (85 g) fresh mozzarella, pinched into small chunks
2 cups (220 g) low-moisture mozzarella, shredded
¼ cup (60 ml) extra-virgin olive oil
½ cup (50 g) coarsely grated Grana Padano cheese
10 fresh basil leaves

Preheat the oven and pizza stone to 500°F (260°C) or, if possible, 550°F (287°C). To make the pizza, first follow the instructions on prepping and rolling out the dough included in the Make & Bake section (page 41). Spread the sauce on your dough. Next, add both mozzarellas and drizzle with about 2 tablespoons of the olive oil. Bake as described in Make & Bake (page 41). When the pie is finished, you'll add the magic. Grate the Grana Padano straight on top of the pie. Don't use the smallest size on your grater. You want more of the medium grate. Next, drizzle with the remaining olive oil. It's a pretty oily pie. That's how he does it. And lastly, snip the basil leaves over the pie. Then slice. I hope you love it as much as I do.

CREMINI MUSHROOM AND PEPPERONI PIZZA

Makes one 14- to 16-inch (35.5- to 40.5-cm) pizza

Listen. My favorite pizzas are either a margherita plain type or a marinara. You can't beat the simplicity. But toppings-wise, this is the number-one pizza combo in my book. Salty, spicy, cured pork with rich, earthy mushrooms. That's all I have to say.

1 ball dough (page 27)
¾ cup (180 ml) tomato sauce (page 33)
3 ounces (85 g) fresh mozzarella, pinched into small chunks
2 cups (220 g) shredded low-moisture mozzarella
2 ounces (55 g) pepperoni, sliced moderately thin
1½ cups (90 g) cremini mushrooms, thinly sliced
Fine sea salt
3 tablespoons grated hard cheese
Dried Sicilian oregano
Extra-virgin olive oil

Preheat the oven and pizza stone to 500°F (260°C) or, if possible, 550°F (287°C). To make the pizza, first follow the instructions on prepping and rolling out the dough included in the Make & Bake section (page 41). Top your dough with the tomato sauce, then both mozzarellas, pepperoni, and the mushrooms last. Sprinkle with a pinch of salt, then bake as described in Make & Bake (page 41). Finish with the grated hard cheese, a pinch of Sicilian oregano, and a drizzle of olive oil.

PISTACHIO PESTO PIZZA

Makes one 14- to 16-inch (35.5- to 40.5-cm) pizza

I love pistachios because they're rich, fatty, and a Sicilian favorite. The lemon zest and juice in this pesto balances the pistachios with acid and freshness. This is a great pizza to add arugula or other salad greens to, as well. This recipe makes more pesto than you'll need, but don't worry, it won't go to waste—it works really well tossed with roasted vegetables or with a hot or cold pasta.

For the pesto:
Makes about 2 cups (480 ml)
2 cups (260 g) shelled pistachios (bonus
  if you find the Sicilian variety)
Zest and juice of 1 lemon
Fistful of fresh basil (20 to 30 large leaves)
1 cup (100 g) freshly grated hard cheese
2 large cloves garlic, pressed or minced
Fine sea salt and freshly ground black pepper
1 cup (240 ml) extra-virgin olive oil, plus more for
  finishing

For the pizza:
1 ball dough (page 27)
3 ounces (85 g) fresh mozzarella, pinched into small
  chunks
2 cups (220 g) shredded low-moisture mozzarella
3 tablespoons grated hard cheese

Put your nuts in a high-powered blender or food processor and chop until fine. Add the lemon zest and juice, basil, 1 cup grated hard cheese, garlic, and salt and pepper to taste, and pulse while slowly adding 1 cup olive oil. Taste and add more salt and pepper as desired.

Preheat the oven and pizza stone to 500°F (260°C) or, if possible, 550°F (287°C). To make the pizza, first follow the instructions on prepping and rolling out the dough included in the Make & Bake section (page 41). Spread 1 cup (240 ml) of the pesto on the dough, going all the way to the edges and being careful not to go over, then add both mozzarellas. Bake as described in Make & Bake (page 41). Finish this pizza with 3 tablespoons grated hard cheese and a drizzle of olive oil.

MARINARA AND ANCHOVY PIZZA

Makes one 14- to 16-inch (35.5- to 40.5-cm) pizza

Some drunk guy invented this pizza. He came in the shop and ordered, "Hold the mozzarella cheese, add garlic and anchovy. The grated cheese is okay, too, but no mozzarella." And then didn't come back to pick it up. That forced me to eat it, and I discovered how great this pizza is. It's much lighter than a regular cheese pie but definitely not less flavorful. You can omit the anchovies, but that would be a mistake.

1 ball dough (page 27)
1½ cups (360 ml) tomato sauce (page 33)
1 or 2 large cloves garlic (or more, if you like), thinly sliced
2 pinches dried Sicilian oregano
3 tablespoons extra-virgin olive oil
½ cup (50 g) or more grated hard cheese
6 to 8 anchovy fillets, cut in half

Preheat the oven and pizza stone to 500°F (260°C) or, if possible, 550°F (287°C). To make the pizza, first follow the instructions on prepping and rolling out the dough included in the Make & Bake section (page 41). Spread the sauce on the dough. Add the garlic, then the oregano, and drizzle with 1 tablespoon of the olive oil. Bake as described in Make & Bake (page 41)—though this pizza normally cooks a minute or two faster than one with cheese. It will also be a little crispier. (Both good things.)

Sprinkle the grated hard cheese over the finished pie. Drizzle with the remaining 2 tablespoons of olive oil. Cut the pizza. Lastly, arrange your anchovies so each slice has one anchovy, adding more if you like.

Cheers to the drunk guy!

SICILIAN ALMOND PESTO PIZZA

Makes one 14- to 16-inch (35.5- to 40.5-cm) pizza

This is a great pesto that I normally toss with hot pasta, which got me thinking that it'd be even better on pizza. I really liked the outcome so I make it all the time now. I'm not sure if this is really Sicilian, but that's what I call it. This isn't a history book.

For the pesto:
Makes about 2 cups (480 ml)

1 cup (140 g) raw unsalted almonds
4 medium tomatoes, quartered
10 basil leaves, plus 3 or 4 torn for finishing
2 cloves garlic, pressed or minced
¼ cup (60 ml) extra-virgin olive oil
1 cup (100 g) grated hard cheese
Fine sea salt and freshly ground black pepper

For the pizza:

1 ball dough (page 27)
3 ounces (85 g) fresh mozzarella, pinched into small chunks
2 cups (220 g) shredded low-moisture mozzarella
3 tablespoons grated hard cheese
Extra-virgin olive oil

Preheat the oven and pizza stone to 500°F (260°C) or, if possible, 550°F (287°C).

In a food processor, combine the almonds, tomatoes, 10 basil leaves, garlic, ¼ cup olive oil, and 1 cup of grated hard cheese. Blend until it seems that there aren't any large chunks. Season to taste with salt and pepper. It will keep in the refrigerator for about 5 days.

To make the pizza, first follow the instructions on prepping and rolling out the dough included in the Make & Bake section (page 41). Spread 2 cups (480 ml) of the pesto on the dough, going all the way to the edges, being careful not to go over. Bake as described in Make & Bake (page 41). Finish this pizza with the remaining torn basil leaves, 3 tablespoons of grated hard cheese, and a drizzle of olive oil.

MORTADELLA, RICOTTA CREAM, ROASTED PEPPER PIZZA

Makes one 14- to 16-inch (35.5- to 40.5-cm) pizza

These are some of my favorite childhood flavors combined on a pizza. They remind me of our family visits to my aunt and uncle in northeast Philly. They always had a big spread of Italian meats and cheeses and such. We didn't have access to the same stuff in suburban Lancaster. About twenty years later I read about this new pizzeria in Chicago that was putting mortadella on a pizza. I had to try one. The place was called Great Lake, and the pizza was amazing! Unfortunately, Great Lake is now closed. So this is my tribute.

1 ball dough (page 27)
⅔ to 1 cup (165 to 240 ml) Ricotta Cream (page 62)
3 ounces (85 g) fresh mozzarella, pinched into small chunks
2 cups (220 g) shredded low-moisture mozzarella
⅔ cup (75 g) chopped or sliced roasted red peppers
6 to 8 paper-thin slices mortadella

Preheat the oven and pizza stone to 500°F (260°C) or, if possible, 550°F (287°C). To make the pizza, first follow the instructions on prepping and rolling out the dough included in the Make & Bake section (page 41). Spread the ricotta cream on your dough. Add both mozzarellas and the roasted red peppers. Bake as described in Make & Bake (page 41). When the pizza comes out of the oven, carefully arrange the mortadella to completely cover everything but the crust. Slice.

I could kiss this pizza.

BREAKFAST PIZZA: SAUSAGE, EGGS, SPINACH, AND CREAM

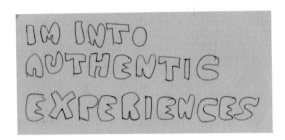

IM INTO AUTHENTIC EXPERIENCES

Makes one 14- to 16-inch (35.5- to 40.5-cm) pizza

Great for breakfast, but to be enjoyed anytime.

The first time I had this pizza was the first time I let my dough sit overnight in the fridge. I woke up excited and didn't want to wait until normal pizza-eating time to make it. I remember how great the flavors in the crust had improved since the previous night's pizza.

This is a cream-based pie, but tomato sauce works well here, too.

1 ball dough (page 27)

3 ounces (85 g) fresh mozzarella, pinched into small chunks

2 cups (220 g) shredded low-moisture mozzarella

2 or 3 handfuls baby spinach

1 large clove garlic, chopped or very thinly sliced

½ cup (70 g) sausage (page 72)

½ cup (120 ml) heavy cream

Fine sea salt

2 large eggs

Freshly ground black pepper

2 tablespoons chopped fresh chives

Crushed red pepper flakes

Extra-virgin olive oil

3 tablespoons grated hard cheese

Preheat the oven and pizza stone to 500°F (260°C) or, if possible, 550°F (287°C). To make the pizza, first follow the instructions on prepping and rolling out the dough included in the Make & Bake section (page 41). Start by adding both mozzarellas to the dough, followed by the spinach and garlic. Add the sausage. Top with the cream and season with salt. Bake as described in Make & Bake (page 41), for 3 minutes, then open the oven, pull out the rack with the baking stone, crack the eggs into the center of the pizza, and season them with salt and pepper. Push the rack back into the oven, close the door, and finish baking. When the pizza is done, remove it from the oven and finish with the chives, a pinch or two of crushed red pepper flakes, a drizzle of olive oil, and the grated hard cheese.

Buenos días!

ASPARAGUS, SPRING CREAM, ONION, LEMON PIZZA

SPRING SPRANG SPRUNG

Makes one 14- to 16-inch (35.5- to 40.5-cm) pizza

The first asparagus of the season is always a treat. Make sure you wash it, as it can be a little sandy. You also need to make sure that you get rid of the woodsy, inedible bottoms. The freshest-cut stuff that you find at the farmers' market is always best. I slice the spears into little coins. The thinner the better.

1 ball dough (page 27)
⅔ cup (165 ml) Spring Cream (page 64)
3 ounces (85 g) fresh mozzarella, pinched into small chunks
2 cups (220 g) shredded low-moisture mozzarella
About 2 cups (270 g) chopped fresh asparagus
Fine sea salt
3 tablespoons grated hard cheese
Extra-virgin olive oil
1 lemon wedge
2 tablespoons chopped fresh chives

Preheat the oven and pizza stone to 500°F (260°C) or, if possible, 550°F (287°C). To make the pizza, first follow the instructions on prepping and rolling out the dough included in the Make & Bake section (page 41). Cover the dough with the spring cream, then add the mozzarellas. Now I like to add a very liberal amount of asparagus. Season with salt. Bake as described in Make & Bake (page 41). Finish with the grated hard cheese, a drizzle of olive oil, a spritz of fresh lemon juice from the wedge, and the chives.

PINEAPPLE, BACON, AND JALAPEÑO PIZZA

Makes one 14- to 16-inch (35.5- to 40.5-cm) pizza

I have a whole list of things that I'd never put on a pizza, but oddly, pineapple ain't one. This is a combination of flavors I love, and rules are meant to be broken, etc., etc. I love how the heat provided by the peppers balances the sweetness of the pineapple. If you don't like it, sue me.

¼ pound (115 g) good smoked slab bacon, cut into lardons and sautéed (page 77)
1 ball dough (page 27)
¾ cup (180 ml) tomato sauce (page 33)
3 ounces (85 g) fresh mozzarella, pinched into small chunks
2 cups (220 g) shredded low-moisture mozzarella
1 cup fresh pineapple, diced
1 jalapeño, sliced
3 tablespoons grated hard cheese
Extra-virgin olive oil

Preheat the oven and pizza stone to 500°F (260°C) or, if possible, 550°F (287°C).

To make the pizza, first follow the instructions on prepping and rolling out the dough included in the Make & Bake section (page 41). Spread the sauce over the dough. Top with both mozzarellas, pineapple, bacon, and jalapeño slices. Bake as described in Make & Bake (page 41), then finish with the grated hard cheese and a drizzle of olive oil.

ZUCCHINI, CREAM, BASIL, AND GARLIC PIZZA

Makes one 14- to 16-inch (35.5- to 40.5-cm) pizza

I just put this one together a week ago, and it was a surprise hit. It's the perfect pizza for midsummer because it uses two of the best mid-summer ingredients—zucchini and basil.

1 medium zucchini, sliced into ⅛-inch-
  (3-mm-) thick coins
Fine sea salt and freshly ground black pepper
1 ball dough (page 27)
1 cup (240 ml) heavy cream
Handful fresh basil leaves (10 to 12 leaves),
  plus more for garnish
1 large clove garlic, minced
3 ounces (85 g) fresh mozzarella,
  pinched into small chunks
2 cups (220 g) shredded low-moisture mozzarella
3 tablespoons grated hard cheese
Extra-virgin olive oil

Season the zucchini coins liberally with salt and pepper, then cover with paper towels and let sit out for about an hour to drain.

Preheat the oven and pizza stone to 500°F (260°C) or, if possible, 550°F (287°C). To make the pizza, first follow the instructions on prepping and rolling out the dough included in the Make & Bake section (page 41). In a food processor, combine the cream, basil, and garlic and blend until slightly emulsified. Spread ½ cup (120 ml) of the basil cream on your dough, then top with both mozzarellas. Blot the zucchini coins, then completely cover the dough from end to end with them. Bake as described in Make & Bake (page 41).

Finish with torn fresh basil, the grated hard cheese, and a drizzle of olive oil.

ROASTED FENNEL AND SAUSAGE PIZZA

Makes one 14- to 16-inch (35.5- to 40.5-cm) pizza

I added sausage to this pizza because (insert sausage joke here).

1 ball dough (page 27)
¾ cup (180 ml) tomato sauce (page 33)
3 ounces (85 g) fresh mozzarella,
    pinched into small chunks
2 cups (220 g) shredded low-moisture mozzarella
1½ cups (90 g) roasted fennel (page 99)
1 cup (140 g) sausage (page 72)
Fine sea salt
3 tablespoons grated hard cheese
Dried Sicilian oregano
Extra-virgin olive oil

Preheat the oven and pizza stone to 500°F (260°C) or, if possible, 550°F (287°C). To make the pizza, first follow the instructions on prepping and rolling out the dough included in the Make & Bake section (page 41). Top your dough with the tomato sauce, both mozzerellas, then the roasted fennel and sausage. Sprinkle with a pinch of salt, then bake as described in Make & Bake (page 41). Finish with the grated hard cheese, a pinch of Sicilian oregano, and a drizzle of olive oil.

STROMBOLI

Makes one 14-inch (35.5-cm) stromboli

This is what I make when I don't want pizza but have some dough laying around. I like to keep it simple, but feel free to fill with whatever ingredients you have. Most of the time I just add fresh mozzarella, tomato sauce, and one additional ingredient, or none at all. The main goal is basically to bake the stromboli without having it oozing all over the place.

1 ball dough (page 27)
¾ cup (180 ml) tomato sauce (page 33)
½ cup (57 g) torn or shredded fresh mozzarella
Extra-virgin olive oil
3 tablespoons grated hard cheese
1 cup (140 g) of cooked sausage or other meat (optional)

Preheat your oven to 450°F (230°C) with the pizza stone on the middle rack.

Stretch your dough on a floured surface. Feel free to use a rolling pin or wine bottle to flatten it. Normally you wouldn't do that with a pizza, but our goals are different here. We want to keep it as even as possible. Stretch the dough into a rectangular shape (about 12 by 14 inches / 30.5 by 35.5 cm). Spread your tomato sauce out, leaving a 2-inch (5-cm) border on all sides. Add the mozzarella, a drizzle of olive oil, and the grated hard cheese. If you'd like some sausage or something, now's the time to add it.

Fold the dough over along one of the long sides and crimp and press the edges to seal. Try to do it as tightly as possible. Gently transfer the stromboli to your floured peel. With a sharp knife, cut tiny slits in the top of the dough to let steam escape. Transfer to the hot stone and bake for 25 to 30 minutes or until golden brown. Remove from the oven and let it rest for 5 to 10 minutes before slicing.

PAN PIZZA

Makes one 10-inch (25-cm) pan pizza

This is like a thick, Sicilian-style pie. It's a little greasy, which makes it rich and delicious. Ideally you will have a 10-inch (25.5-cm) round cast-iron skillet to cook it in, but you can also use a quarter sheet pan. The crust essentially fries in the olive-oil-coated skillet, making the pizza turn out wonderful and crunchy.

2 tablespoons extra-virgin olive oil,
   plus 1 for finishing
1 ball dough (page 27)
¾ cup (180 ml) tomato sauce (page 33)
3 ounces (85 g) fresh mozzarella,
   pinched into small chunks
2 cups (220 g) shredded low-moisture mozzarella
3 to 4 ounces (85 to 115 g) sliced pepperoni
Pinch or two dried Sicilian oregano
3 tablespoons grated hard cheese

Preheat the oven to 500°F (260°C) or, if possible, 550°F (287°C). Oil your cast-iron pan with 2 tablespoons of olive oil. Stretch your dough to fit into the pan that you're using. Top the dough with your tomato sauce and both mozzarella cheeses. Add the pepperoni. For some reason, when I go to Di Fara I like to ask for pepperoni on this one. (Di Fara does two types: a round traditional New York–style pizza and a square pan-style pizza.) It's kind of indulgent. Place the pan on the middle rack of your oven and bake until well done, 8 to 12 minutes.

Finish with a drizzle of olive oil, the oregano, and the grated hard cheese. Make sure you pull it out of what you baked it in and cut it on a cutting board. Don't ruin your pans.

PART
FIVE:
HOAGIES,
SANDWICHES,
ETC.

I've turned my pizza dough into bread when I didn't sell all my pizzas. Sometimes I would go to the deli and get good cold cuts and cheese and make what we in Philadelphia call a hoagie.

"Hoagie" is both an ugly and a beautiful word. It generally refers to a sandwich of Italian meats and cheeses on a long roll, usually with a sturdy crust that is sometimes coated with sesame seeds. You probably call it a sub or a hero. It doesn't matter; you get the point. They are only really good when the bread is good.

If you made this bread and these sandwiches and opened a shop in whatever town you live in, it would be the best sandwich shop in that town. (Unless you live in New York and have access to No. 7 Sub.) Normally I don't brag, but I'm obviously bragging here. Someone prove me wrong.

The process of preparing dough for a hoagie roll is not too much different than preparing dough for pizza. Follow the same process detailed on page 27, but when it comes time to portion the dough into rounds, instead separate them into 12-inch (30.5-cm) lengths, about 3 to 4 inches (7.5 to 10 cm) across. Score the top of each roll and allow them to sit out for 15 to 20 minutes before baking in a 450°F (230°C) oven for 20 to 30 minutes.

Whenever you make a hoagie, don't forget to pull out the doughy insides, leaving mostly the crust, before loading in ingredients. Remember when Rodney Dangerfield made that giant sandwich in *Back to School*? That's pretty much how I roll with my rolls. Sorry.

Italian Hoagie

Makes 1 hoagie

Building a sandwich is a complicated endeavor that is usually done poorly. The key is all about proportions and seasonings. The meats need to be sliced thin, the cheese sliced thin to medium, the roll dressed evenly and liberally, and do not forget to season your vegetables. I hate eating a sandwich with a big beautiful slice of tomato that doesn't pop like it should. Adding just a bit of salt and pepper goes a long way and really brings it all together. In Philly, an Italian hoagie is usually dressed with a vinaigrette or just oil and vinegar. The problem is that no one uses decent olive oil. The grassiness or fruitiness of a decent extra-virgin olive oil takes it to the next level.

1 hoagie roll (page 172)
Extra-virgin olive oil
4 to 6 thin slices American cheese or
    Italian provolone cheese
6 thin slices mortadella
6 thin slices capicola
2 tablespoons pickled chiles
Thinly sliced white onion (optional)
Sliced tomato (optional)
Fine sea salt and freshly ground black pepper
Dried Sicilian oregano
2 cups (40 g) arugula

I start by slicing the roll lengthwise, being careful not to go the whole way through. It's just easier to eat and less messy it if it's closed on one side. Take your olive oil (with your thumb partially covering the opening) and dress the roll with a couple of tablespoons. Take care to distribute the oil evenly. Next add the slices of cheese, overlapping each piece by about an inch (2.5 cm).

Next add the mortadella. Make sure that it's been cut paper thin. Drape about six slices over the cheese. I like to loop it back over itself. Making it "nice." Then add the capicola. Capicola is traditionally made with the shoulder or the neck of the pig and slow-cured, sometimes with spices; I recommend you get the spicy version. Drape the capicola over the mortadella. Next put on some pickled chiles. This will give the hoagie some nice heat and acid. Onions and tomatoes are optional. This is when you'd add them; just hit them with a little salt and pepper. I like a small pinch of Sicilian oregano, too. Lastly, toss some arugula with a little olive oil and spread a medium-size pile on top of the hoagie. Take a long knife and cram the greens down while closing the hoagie with your other hand carefully. Turn the hoagie on its side and press down again while slicing it on a bias.

Hoagie Additions:

I like roasted peppers (page 98), if you have them. A few slices will do. I also really love long hot roasted peppers (page 90). They can be really spicy, so one or two whole peppers should be sufficient. Substitute the long hots for the pickled chiles. And lastly, controversially, you can put mayo on an Italian hoagie. Somebody will probably get mad about this, but who cares.

Roasted Veggie Hoagie

Makes 4 hoagies

This is the trifecta of Italian roasted vegetables with provolone and a homemade dressing. A thick slice of eggplant, sautéed broccoli rabe or spinach with garlic, and roasted peppers make a hell of a sandwich.

For the dresing:

3 large cloves garlic, pressed or minced
¾ cup (180 ml) mayonnaise
Zest and juice of 1 lemon
4 anchovy fillets packed in oil
Fat pinch dried Sicilian oregano
Fat pinch crushed red pepper flakes
Extra-virgin olive oil
¼ cup (13 g) chopped fresh Italian parsley or chives
Fine sea salt and freshly ground black pepper
1 medium eggplant

For the hoagies:

1 bunch broccoli rabe
1 large clove garlic, thinly sliced
4 hoagie rolls (page 172), split not entirely
8 slices provolone cheese
1 cup (175 g) sliced roasted red peppers
4 roasted long hots (optional, page 90)

Preheat the oven to 450°F (230°C).

The homemade dressing is easy. In a food processor, combine the pressed garlic, mayonnaise, lemon zest and juice, anchovies, oregano, red pepper flakes, 2 tablespoons olive oil, parsley or chives, and salt and pepper to taste. Refrigerate for at least 20 minutes before using.

Cut the eggplant in half lengthwise. Score the cut sides in a crisscross pattern, being careful not to cut too deep. Liberally coat the scored side with olive oil and season with salt and pepper. Place the eggplant on a rimmed baking sheet, cut sides up, and bake for 30 to 40 minutes. The eggplant should have good color. Let cool.

For the broccoli rabe, heat a large skillet over medium heat with 3 tablespoons of olive oil. Add the sliced garlic and sauté until just starting to brown, about 2 minutes. Just don't burn the garlic. Remove the garlic from the pan. Take your broccoli rabe and separate the leaves and florets from any thick stems. Chop the stems into ½-inch (12-mm) pieces and add them and the rest of the rabe to the pan. Add a couple pinches of salt, cover, and cook for about 20 minutes or until the rabe is wilted.

To build the sandwich, spread 2 to 3 tablespoons of the dressing on each roll. Put a couple of provolone slices down next. Cut each eggplant half into quarters lengthwise and add two quarters to each hoagie. Divide the rabe among the hoagies and top with the roasted peppers. If you're feeling frisky, add a roasted long hot to each sandwich. Squeeze tight and cut in half.

Meatball Hoagie

Makes 10 to 12 hoagies

These are pretty good meatballs. You can trust me—you've gotten this far in the book.

A few tips:
- The meatballs mix better when you whisk the milk and breadcrumbs. It makes something that looks like a porridge and incorporates well.
- I like to shape the meatballs into patties. They do this at Parm in NYC. It's really smart because when you put regular meatballs in a sandwich they tend to fall out or squeeze out. It never happens with a patty.

Extra-virgin olive oil
2 cups (200 g) dry breadcrumbs (page 205)
1 cup (240 ml) whole milk
4 pounds (1.8 kg) coarsely or medium ground veal, pork, and beef
½ pound (250 g) provolone cheese, finely grated
2 pounds (910 g) ricotta cheese
4 large eggs
2 large garlic cloves, grated with a Microplane
2 tablespoons fine sea salt
8 cups (2 L) Tomato Sauce (page 33)
10 to 12 hoagie rolls (8 to 12 inches long), split
30 to 40 slices provolone cheese
1 cup (125 g) grated hard cheese, for finishing

Oil two or three large baking sheets and preheat your oven to 450°F (230°C).

Whisk your breadcrumbs in with your milk in your largest mixing bowl. Add the ground meat, ricotta, eggs, garlic, and salt to the bowl and mix with your hands until everything looks incorporated. You can take a large pinch and fry it in a pan to see if the meatball mixture needs a seasoning adjustment.

Scoop out ⅓ to ½ cup (65 to 100 g) of the meat mixture for each meatball, place them on the prepared baking sheets, and flatten them into patties. Working in batches if necessary, bake the patties for 15 minutes, then flip them and bake for another 5 to 10 minutes until they are browned and cooked through. Let rest.

Pour the tomato sauce into a large, wide Dutch oven and add the meatball patties. Simmer over medium-low heat for about 20 minutes or until everything is heated through and the sauce has reduced a bit.

Lightly toast your rolls. Lay 3 or 4 slices of provolone in each roll, then add 3 or 4 meatballs and some sauce to cover. Top each hoagie with a heaping tablespoon of the grated hard cheese just before serving.

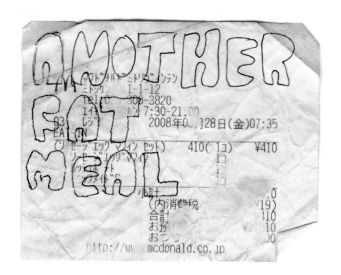

Roast Pork Sandwich

Makes 6 to 8 sandwiches

Don't believe what you've been told. This is the real star in the Philadelphia sandwich world. It's much more dynamic than the cheesesteak in my opinion. This pork recipe will make more than you need—feel free to share or freeze the leftovers. It's a two-part process. We dry brine the pork shoulder overnight and roast it for a few hours the next day. It's not a lot of work, it's just a decent amount of time. The pork is so tender and juicy it will be worth all of your efforts.

3 to 4 sprigs fresh rosemary, chopped
1 tablespoon fennel seeds
1 tablespoon red pepper flakes
6 to 8 cloves garlic
2 tablespoons kosher salt
1 tablespoon black pepper
½ cup (120 ml) extra-virgin olive oil
1 (5- to 7-pound / 2.3- to 3.2-kg) boneless
   pork shoulder
6 to 8 hoagie rolls (page 172), split not entirely
6 to 8 cups (930 g to 1.2 kg) sautéed
   spinach with garlic
12 to 16 slices provolone cheese
6 to 8 roasted long hots (optional, page 90)

Start by making a paste with the rosemary, fennel seeds, red pepper flakes, garlic (use a garlic press or mortar and pestle to crush the cloves), salt, pepper, and olive oil. Massage mixture all over your meat. Cover and refrigerate for 12 to 24 hours. If you're in a bind, you could let it sit for a couple hours before you roast it, but waiting makes it better.

Preheat the oven to 450°F (230°C). Place the pork in a large Dutch oven or cast-iron pot. Bake for 40 minutes, then reduce the heat to 325°F (165°C) and cover the pot. Continue to cook for another 3 hours, or until you can pull the pork apart easily. Let cool. With clean hands, shred the meat. Add the shredded meat back into the jus and keep warm.

To build the sandwich, pile about 1½ cups (295 g) shredded pork with its juice on each hoagie roll. Distribute the spinach and provolone slices evenly over the sandwiches. Finish with a long hot if you like some extra heat. Enjoy this Philly classic.

COME TO FISHTOWN TONIGHT
IF YOU WANT TO SEE BROS
MATING IN THEIR NATURAL HABITAT

Oxtail Hoagie

Makes 4 to 6 hoagies

This is a good sandwich to eat in the dead of winter. It's rich and may require a nap after consuming. Oxtail is just beef, so don't get all weird on me. To be honest, oxtails are delicious but are a bit of a pain in the ass to work with because of the bone and cartilage. Once they're braised it's really easy to pull the meat off, though. So if you're up for the challenge and really want to impress your friends, this is a great recipe. I've also added a spicy mayo spread that goes great with the oxtail.

For the oxtail:

3 tablespoons vegetable oil, or other neutral oil
5 pounds (2.3 kg) oxtails
Fine sea salt and freshly ground black pepper
1 large sweet onion, chopped
2 cups (280 g) peeled and chopped carrots
    (about 1 pound / 455 g)
2 cups (200 g) chopped celery (about 6 stalks)
1 (6-ounce / 170-g) can tomato paste
1 head of garlic, cloves peeled and chopped
1 (750 ml) bottle dry red wine (something that you'd
    actually drink)
4 cups (960 ml) chicken stock or water
2 bay leaves

For the spicy mayo:

2 tablespoons extra-virgin olive oil
2 shallots, chopped
3 cloves garlic, thinly sliced
2 long hots, chopped
1 cup (240 ml) mayonnaise
10 basil leaves
Fine sea salt

For the sandwiches:

4 to 6 hoagie rolls (page 172), split not entirely
½ pound (225 g) (or more) Piave cheese, grated
4 to 6 handfuls arugula

To make the oxtails: Pat your oxtails dry with paper towels. Season liberally with salt and pepper. Cover and refrigerate for a couple hours or overnight.

Preheat the oven to 325°F (165°C).

Pour a few tablespoons of neutral oil into a Dutch oven or heavy soup pot set over medium-high heat. Working in batches, sear the oxtails on all sides, then transfer to a plate. Cook the onion in the pan drippings until just colored, 5 to 7 minutes. Add the carrots and celery and cook until softened, 6 to 8 minutes. Add the tomato paste and chopped garlic, cook for 1 to 2 minutes, stirring constantly, then pour in the wine and stock. Add the oxtails back to the pot and toss in the bay leaves. Transfer to the oven and cook for 3 to 3½ hours, or until the meat is easily pulled from the bones with a fork. Remove the pot from the oven and let it cool.

To make the mayo: Heat the oil in a large skillet over medium-high heat. Add the shallots, garlic, and long hots and sauté for 5 to 7 minutes, or until the garlic begins to brown. Remove the pan from the heat and let it cool slightly, then scrape the mixture into a food processor, along with the mayo and basil leaves. Process until smooth, then season with salt to taste. Cover and refrigerate until ready to use.

Skim the fat from the top of the oxtail pot and place the oxtails on a platter. Use a slotted spoon to remove any solids from the pot. Pull the meat off the bones and place the meat back into the liquid.

To construct the sandwiches: Spread 2 tablespoons of spicy mayo on each roll. Add some grated Piave cheese, then spoon on some warm oxtail with some of its juices. Top with arugula.

Pepper + Egg Breakfast Hoagie

Makes 1 hoagie

This is a perfect start to your day if you like sandwiches. It will keep you satiated until late afternoon, and you can get your shit done. I also like some serious heat with my eggs, so I will add a chopped long hot or two to my roasted pepper mixture. If you can't handle the heat, leave the long hots out and it will still make for a great sandwich.

4 large eggs, whisked
1 to 2 tablespoons heavy cream or milk
Fine sea salt and freshly ground black pepper
2 tablespoons unsalted butter
½ cup (72 g) chopped roasted bell peppers
    (page 98)
½ cup (72 g) long hots (page 90)
Extra-virgin olive oil
1 hoagie roll (page 172), split not entirely

It's a little like making a frittata. Whisk four good eggs with the cream, then add a pinch of salt and a couple turns of pepper.

Place the butter in a large, nonstick skillet. Add your roasted peppers and long hots to the pan to heat them up. Once the peppers have warmed, pour the egg mixture over them. Don't mess around with the eggs. Let them set before touching them. Once the eggs have started to set, turn the heat down to low and flip the eggs. Continue to cook for an additional minute, then turn off the heat.

I like to drizzle some good olive oil into my roll. Then transfer the pepper and egg mixture into the roll using a spatula. And if you're using a day-old roll, don't forget to toast it in the oven for a few minutes—this will bring the bread back to life.

Smoked Salmon Hoagie

Makes 1 hoagie

This is my other breakfast sandwich. Who doesn't crave cured salmon in the morning? It's rich but still feels relatively healthy. A Jewish deli's lox or smoked salmon is always going to be better than what you'll get at a grocery store.

3 to 4 tablespoons cream cheese
1 hoagie roll (page 172), split not entirely
⅓ pound (150 g) thinly sliced smoked salmon (lox)
1 ripe tomato, thinly sliced
1 small red onion, thinly sliced
1 small cucumber, thinly sliced
Fine sea salt and freshly ground black pepper
Sprig or 2 of fresh dill (optional)

Schmear the cream cheese inside the roll, then drape the sliced salmon on one side. Add the sliced veggies and season with salt and pepper. Tuck in the dill sprigs if you have them.

Squeeze tight, slice, share, enjoy.
Good morning.

Cheesesteak

Makes 2 cheesesteaks

Yo! This is the sandwich that put Philadelphia on the map, but honestly most of the high-volume places use crappy meat. I refuse to serve that kind of conventional stuff to my friends and customers, let alone eat it myself. This may be a bougie version of a cheese-steak, but at least it isn't dog meat. I go to my butcher and buy local grass-fed, thinly sliced bottom or top round beef. It's cleaner and nicer and tastes great.

As far as cheese goes, I'd recommend any type of mild white cheese over any sort of processed whiz crap. That ain't cheese, and probably gives you cancer. Who knows what's in that?

1½ pounds (680 g) thinly sliced grass-fed bottom or top round beef
Fine sea salt and freshly ground black pepper
1 tablespoon canola oil
½ pound (225 g) sliced American cheese
⅔ cup (60 g) roasted onions (optional, page 85)
2 hoagie rolls (page 172), split not entirely

Season your steak with salt and pepper. Place a large skillet with the oil over medium-high heat. Add the steak and sauté until it's mostly browned but still a little pink in the middle, 3 to 5 minutes. Drape the cheese slices over the steak and remove the pan from the heat. If you like roasted onions, add them to your roll. With a spatula, transfer half of the cheesesteak mixture to each roll. That is a cheesesteak. It's good. After you digest it, run up the steps of your local museum or library. You're a Philadelphian now.

PHILADELPHIA: I FUCKING LOVE IT HERE.™

Heirloom Tomato Hoagie

Makes 1 hoagie

Here is another treasure of pure simplicity. If your tomatoes are perfect, as in ripe and in season, then you'll never need lettuce and bacon to make them great. The point is to keep it on the lighter side and enjoy the summer's bounty.

2 medium heirloom tomatoes
Fine sea salt and freshly ground black pepper
1 hoagie roll (page 172), split not entirely
4 to 6 tablespoons (60 to 90 ml) real mayonnaise, or more as desired

Cut your heirlooms into 1-inch- (2.5-cm-) wide slices and put them on a plate. Season liberally with salt and pepper. Generously coat both sides of the bread with real mayonnaise. Don't use light mayo or some weird substitute. If you hate mayo, I guess you could use some good olive oil, but that's a different sandwich, man. Arrange the thick-cut tomatoes on your roll, and pour on any liquid that is left on the plate.

Press, slice, enjoy.

Smoked Sardine Hoagie

Makes 1 hoagie

A can of smoked sardines has much more flavor than any can of tuna and is a rather healthy sandwich option. I don't have a lot to write about this as a sandwich other than that I eat it often and I love it. What else do you want?

1 ripe avocado
Zest and juice of 1 lemon
2 tablespoons extra-virgin olive oil
Fine sea salt and freshly ground black pepper
1 (4.5-ounce / 130 g) can smoked sardines
   or kippers
1 serrano chile, stemmed and finely chopped
   (not seeded)
½ cup (25 g) chopped fresh Italian parsley
½ cup (65 g) finely chopped red onion
1 hoagie roll (page 172), split not entirely

In a medium bowl, mash the avocado flesh with a fork. Add the lemon zest and juice and olive oil, stir well, and season to taste with salt and pepper.

Drain the sardines or kippers and place them in a medium mixing bowl. There shouldn't be any bones or anything, but I always check. Again, I like everything pretty spicy, so here I like to add a finely chopped serrano pepper, seeds and all. Add the parsley and red onion to the bowl, toss well, and season with salt and pepper to taste. Spread the mashed avocado inside the roll. Fill with the sardine salad. Squeeze, slice, enjoy, dog.

Tomato Bread

Makes 1 loaf

Oddly, this is the only recipe in the book with olives in it. I don't love olives cooked, but with the tomato-garlic mixture, when it cools it's really good. Like a tapenade bread thing.

1 ball dough (page 27)
1¼ cups (300 ml) tomato sauce (page 33)
½ cup (75 g) chopped kalamata olives
1 clove garlic, sliced

Preheat the oven to 450°F (230°C).

Stretch out the dough ball to about 14 inches (35.5 cm) in diameter. Spread on the tomato sauce, leaving about a 2-inch (5-cm) border at the edge. Evenly distribute the olives and garlic over the sauce. Starting at the bottom of the dough, lightly roll upward, being careful not to squish any of the sauce or toppings out of the sides. Bake for 30 minutes.

Sausage Bread

Makes 1 loaf

Leftover dough plus sausage equals sausage bread. It's the kind of thing I used to eat at my aunt Anna's. Sometimes there would be yellow mustard inside. It was weird at first, but quite good. I like to use really spicy Dijon, though either works great. Depends on which way you swing.

1 ball dough (page 27)
3 tablespoons yellow or Dijon mustard
½ pound (225 g) cooked sausage
2 tablespoons extra-virgin olive oil

Preheat the oven to 450°F (230°C).

Stretch out the dough ball to about 14 inches (35.5 cm) in diameter. Using a spoon, spread the mustard evenly across the dough, leaving about a 2-inch (5-cm) border at the edge. Sprinkle pieces of sausage evenly over the mustard, then drizzle with the olive oil. Starting at the bottom of the dough, lightly roll upward, being careful not to squish any of the toppings out of the sides. Bake for 30 minutes.

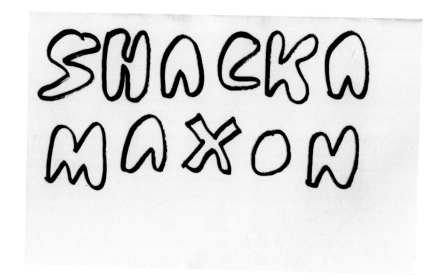

Croutons

Makes 6 to 8 cups (720 to 960 g)

Croutons are for salads. Salads are for people who like to eat vegetables or for people who think they're on a diet. "Crouton" sounds French. They are crunchy cubes of bread seasoned with stuff and can be quite delicious.

½ cup (120 ml) extra-virgin olive oil
2 anchovy fillets
2 cloves garlic
Fat pinch of dried Sicilian oregano
Pinch of crushed red pepper flakes (optional)
1 loaf of day-old bread, cut into small cubes
   (6 to 8 cups / 720 to 960 g)
½ cup (50 g) finely grated hard cheese
Fine sea salt

Preheat the oven to 350°F (175°C).

Heat the olive oil in a large skillet over medium heat, then add the anchovies, garlic, oregano, and crushed red pepper. Cook for 5 minutes, then discard the garlic. Add the bread cubes to the skillet and toss well to coat them in the oil. Spread the coated bread on a rimmed baking sheet in a single layer and bake for 10 minutes. Sprinkle on your grated hard cheese and bake for a few more minutes or until golden. Season with salt to taste.

Breadcrumbs

Makes 1 to 4 cups (125 to 500 g)

What do you think we do with day-old bread? We make breadcrumbs. Take your old bread and tear it into pieces and add them to your food processor. Pulse until it looks like rice. Seal and store in the refrigerator for a few weeks. They add great texture to pasta and salads.

A lot of times I like to season the breadcrumbs before I use them. Melt a tablespoon of butter with a tablespoon of extra-virgin olive oil over medium heat, add one thinly sliced clove of garlic, a fat pinch of crushed red pepper, and a pinch of oregano. Discard the garlic after it has lightly toasted. Add 1 cup (100 g) of bread crumbs and cook until toasty and crunchy, about 10 minutes. Season with salt.

PHILLY FOOD FRIENDS

This is really such a great town. It's an opinion not shared by all, but it's been my experience. It's an honest town in that you know where you stand and what someone thinks of you. I find that refreshing—to be judged on how you treat people and your character. There is a diehard type of loyalty in Philadelphia that I've never seen anywhere else.

It may take a minute to crack the shell, so to speak, but after Philadelphians know you, they'll invite you into their homes and into their lives. From where I'm standing as a human being, Philadelphia is a wonderful thing.

I feel really fortunate to be part of this fabric.

At the very least, this is where America started. Benjamin Franklin was one of America's first free thinkers and a great inventor. (I really have no idea what I'm talking about.)

Here, in pictures, are some of my favorite food spots and more importantly, the people who run them. These are friends that I'm proud of and places that inspire me. This is less than 5 percent of the rich community that will cook your food and serve your drinks when you come to Philadelphia, but it will have to do in terms of this book. These are people that I would die for if I were in the army and I wasn't such a pussy.

Nick Macri, La Divisa Meats:

This dude comes from Canada, from a long line of southern Italians who've cured and butchered their own meat. He's got a long red beard, a big dog, just lost some weight, and has an attractive wife. Nick's sausage is the best I've ever had, which doesn't include his cured meats and butchered cuts. He's in the Reading Terminal Market, which is a Philadelphia landmark that you must visit. Go spend some money there, but don't tell him I sent you.

READING
TERMINAL
MARKET

FILBERT STREET FLOWER MARKET

In loving memory of Michael J. Holahan

May · June · July · August · Sept.
21 · 25 · 30 · 27 · 24

10 am - 4 pm

ReadingTerminalMarket.org

Pat O'Malley and Scott Schroeder, Hungry Pigeon:

Pat makes the best pastries in Philadelphia. Scott is a solid scrappy cook and dates my sister. I had to include him. JK. Scott is really one of the best cooks in town. He uses the freshest local meats and produce and gives them lots of love.

Joey Baldino, Zeppoli:

I love Zeppoli. It's my favorite restaurant in Philly and the place that I would go for my last meal. It feels like real Sicily and tastes as good, if not better. I recommend making a reservation for four to six people and letting the kitchen cook for you. If you order, then you have to make choices. Let Joey decide.

Chadd Jenkins, Little Fish:

I used to work for Chadd. Not usually a fan of guys named Chad (or Chadd), but he's okay. The best seafood in town that is both rustic and well thought out. He is also part of my favorite Philadelphia family. Hi Vivian, Thelma, and Robynn!

FISHTOWN

Shigeru (Rue) Fukuyoshi and Chizuko Fukuyoshi, Sagami:

I can always eat here. This dude opened right over the bridge in Jersey in 1974, and is still behind the counter. He's got to be in his mid- to late seventies. There is no greater Japanese food in this area in regards to consistency and dedication. Sagami is not fancy or modern (thank God), but it is the most honest Japanese food that I've ever had stateside. Just don't go and only order sushi because all the non-sushi food is excellent. The sushi rice is also great. I'd also like to thank Rue's wife, Chizuko, for holding it all together.

Aaron Ultimo, Ultimo Coffee:

Aaron is a coffee savant. I love to watch some-one operate who clearly cares as much as he does. I don't live near his cafés, so I don't visit as often as I'd like, but I do go out of my way when I can. He even started roasting his own beans. Sounds like a lot of work. If you're in my neighborhood, I'd highly recommend ReAnimator Coffee, which is also excellent.

Other excellent Philadelphia food and drink friends:

Vernick Food & Drink, Stock, Philly Style Bagels, Russet, Square Pie, Capofitto, High Street on Market, Cheu Noodle Bar, Zahav/Dizengoff/Abe Fisher/Federal Donuts, Le Virtu, Stargazy, Fountain Porter, Fishtown Tavern (this is the dive bar by my house), Kensington Quarters, a.kitchen, V Street, Vedge, SPTR and American Sardine Bar, Mr. Joe's Cafe, Tria, and Vetri. There are a lot left off this list. My apologies. xo

SIGNING OFF.

ABOUT THE AUTHOR

Joe Beddia is the owner of Pizzeria Beddia
in Philadelphia, named the best pizza in
America by *Bon Appetit*. Prior to opening
his shop, Beddia made pizzas around Philly
and brewed beer at the Kiuchi Brewery
in Japan.

I'M A VERY, VERY THOUGHTFUL IDIOT.

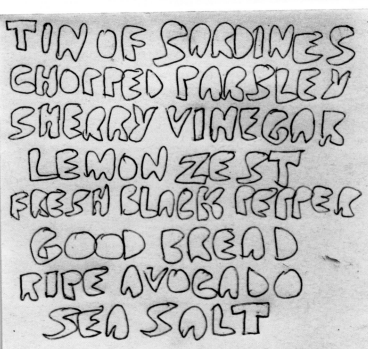

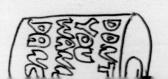

ACKNOWLEDGMENTS

Writing a book is a pain in the ass, and so am I.

I am so thankful to have an insanely smart and patient editor like Camaren Subhiyah. Thank you for taking all the things out of my head and putting them together again. Thank you for working nights and weekends on this book. You deserve a fat promotion and free pizza for life.

I'd also like to thank:

John Gall, for art directing this book with incredible talent and humor.

Walter Green, for designing this book and getting my crazy vision. And going through rounds of what probably seemed like endless revisions. You're awesome.

To my sister, Maria Beddia, thank you for helping me at every turn. Find her at mariatinabeddia.com

A very special thank you to Andrew Knowlton for his early and continued support and for seeing something in me that's always been there. The next round is on me, dude.

Chad Crisp and Drew Lazor, thanks for knowing all the right words and helping me not sound like a total asshole.

John Walker, you're the only guy I trust with the keys to my shop (just look at that face on page 135).

Peggy Paul, for all the pizza-testing and making sure this book will pass pizza school.

Randy Harris, you are a truly talented photographer and absolute nutcase. These photos would be so boring without you.

Barbara Botting, for styling the shit out of our shoot.

Gabriel Levinson, for hunting me down on all my missed deadlines.

True Sims and Anet Sirna-Bruder, for all the behind-the-scenes production work.

Clare Pelino, the best agent in Philly. If you have a restaurant near me, look her up.

Michael Jacobs and Michael Sand, you let me into Abrams. I hope you never kick me out.

INDEX

A

anchovies, 78, 79, 84, *142,*
143, 179, 204
Arrabbiata Pizza, *108,* 109
arugula, 80, 94, 141, 177, *186,*
187
Asparagus, Spring Cream,
Onion, Lemon Pizza, 154,
155

B

bacon, *76, 77,* 115, 156, *157*
basil, 19, 33, 109, 112, *113,*
161
Bintje Potato, Cream, and Rosemary Pizza, *114,* 115
breads. *See also* dough
Breadcrumbs, 205
for hoagies, 172, *174-75*
Sausage Bread, 201
Tomato Bread, 200
Breakfast Pizza: Sausage, Eggs,
Spinach, and Cream, *150,*
151, *152-53*
broccoli, 94, 179
Broccoli, Charred Onion
Cream, and Chile Pizza,
132, 133

C

chard, 94, 130, *131*
cheese, 38. *See also* mozzarella
Fontina, 124
Grana Padano, 39, 137
Parmigiano, 39, 53, 80
Pecorino, 39
in pizza making and baking,
46, *46, 47*
Ricotta Cream, 62, 134, 148,
149

Cheesesteak, *194,* 195
collard greens, 65, 94, 124,
125-26
corn, 112, *113*
creams, 59. *See also* pesto;
sauces
Calabrian Chile Cream, 65,
65, 127, *128-29*
Charred Onion Cream, *132,*
133
English Pea Purée, 65, *65*
Ricotta Cream, 62, 134, 148,
149
Roasted Mushroom Cream,
62, *62*
Roasted or Fresh Garlic
Cream, 64, *64,* 130, *131*
Spring Cream, 64, *64, 120,*
121, *122-23,* 154, *155*
Cremini Mushroom and Pep-
peroni Pizza, 149
Croutons, 204

D

Dandelion Greens, Calabrian
Chile Cream, and Roasted
Red Pepper Pizza, *126,*
127, *128-29*
Dinosaur Kale, Pickled Red
Onion, and Spring Cream
Pizza, *120,* 121, *122-23*
dough, 27, *28,* 29, *30-31,* 43,
43
dressings
Hoagie Dressing, 179
Spicy Mayo, 187

E

English Pea Purée, 65, *65*
equipment, 24-25, *24-26,* 49

F

fennel, 64, 72, *101,* 185
Roasted Fennel, 99, 162, *163*
fiddleheads, 91
flour, 27

G

garlic, 91, 134, 161
garlic press, *25,* 33, 64, 185
Roasted or Fresh Garlic
Cream, 64, *64,* 130, *131*
Great Lake, 19, 23, 148
greens, 94, 96, 127, *128-29.*
See also specific greens

H

half-sours, 88
hoagies
bread for, 172, *174-75*
Heirloom Tomato Hoagie,
196, 197
Hoagie Dressing, 179
Italian Hoagie, *176,* 177
Meatball Hoagie, *182,* 183
Oxtail Hoagie, *186,* 187
Pepper + Egg Breakfast Hoa-
gie, *190,* 191
Roasted Veggie Hoagie, *178,*
179
Smoked Salmon Hoagie, *192,*
193
Smoked Sardine Hoagie, *198,*
199

K

kale, 65, 94, *120*, 121, *122-23*

M

Marinara and Anchovy Pizza, *142*, 143
Mortadella, 80, *82*
  Mortadella, Ricotta Cream, Roasted Pepper Pizza, 148, *149*
mozzarella, 22, 59
  fresh, 19, 39, 46
  low-moisture, 39, 46
  whole milk, 15, 23
mushrooms, 63, 64, 70, *117*, 149
  Roasted Mushroom Cream, 62, *62*, 116
  Sautéed Mushrooms, 84, 116
mustard, 94, 201

O

olive oil, 15, 19, 22, 23, 52, 53
onions, *120*, *122-23*, 154
  Charred Onion Cream, *132*, 133
  Quick Pickling Onions, 85, 121
  Roasted Onions, 85, 195
oregano, 15, 33, *54*
  Sicilian, 53, 140, 143, 162, 168, 177, 179, 204

P

Pan Pizza, 168, *169*
peppers, 65, *65*, *100*, *132*, 133, 156, *157*
  long hots, 90, *92*, 177
  Pickled Chiles, 88, *89*, 177
  Roasted Peppers, 98, 127, *128-29*, 148, *149*, 177
pesto, 24
  Pistachio Pesto, 141
  Sicilian Almond Pesto, 146, *147*
Pineapple, Bacon, and Jalapeño Pizza, 156, *157*
Pistachio Pesto Pizza, 141
pizza, making and baking
  adding cheese, 46, *46*, 47, 53, 54

baking until done, 49, *49-51*, *50-51*
  grand finale in, *52*, 53, *54*, 55
  pizza station set up, 41
  placing in oven, 48, *48*
  removing from oven, 49, *49*
  shaping pie, 42, *42*
  spreading sauce, *44-45*, 45
  stretching dough, 43, *43*
Pizzeria Beddia, 22, 39, 41
  cream added at, 59
  greens at, 94
  olive oil at, 53
  opening of, 19, 23
potatoes, *114*, 115
prosciutto, 80, *81*

R

Rainbow Chard and Roasted Garlic Cream Pizza, 130, *131*
ramps, 91
Ricotta Cream, 62, 134, 148, *149*
Roasted Corn, Heirloom Cherry Tomato, Basil Pizza, 112, *113*
Roasted Fennel and Sausage Pizza, 162, *163*
Roasted Mushroom Cream, 62, *62*, 116
Roasted Mushroom Pizza, 116, *117*
Roasted or Fresh Garlic Cream, 64, *64*, 130, *131*
Roast Pork Sandwich, *184*, 185
rosemary, 62, 80, *114*, 115, 185

S

salames, 65, 74, *75*
salmon, *192*, *193*
sardines, *198*, 199
sauces, 24
  Marinara and Anchovy Pizza, *142*, 143
  Tomato Sauce, 33, *34-37*, 162, *166*, 167
sausage, *71*, *73*, 149, *150*, 151, *152-53*, 162, *163*
  Mortadella, 80, *82*, 148, *149*

Pizzeria Beddia's Sausage, 72
  salames, 74, *75*
  Sausage Bread, 201
  Uncle Pete's Sausage, 70, 72
Sicilian Almond Pesto Pizza, 146, *147*
speck, 80, *83*
  Speck, Collard Greens, Fontina, and Cream Pizza, 124, *125*
Spicy Mayo, 187
spinach, 94, *150*, 151, *152-53*
  Spinach, Ricotta Cream, and Garlic Pizza, 134
Spring Cream, 64, *64*, *120*, 121, *122-23*, 154, *155*
Stromboli, *166*, 167

T

tomatoes, 112, *113*, *196*, 197
  Jersey Fresh, 33
  San Marzano, 19, 23, 33
  Tomato Bread, 200
  Tomato Sauce, 33, *34-37*, 162, *166*, 167
truffles, 95, 97

W

White Pizza, 61
wine, *56*, 57

Z

Zucchini, Cream, Basil, and Garlic Pizza, 161

EDITOR: Camaren Subhiyah
DESIGNER: Walter Green
PRODUCTION MANAGER: True Sims
PHOTO STYLING: Barbara Botting

Library of Congress Control Number:
2016942236

ISBN: 978-1-4197-2409-1

Printed and bound in the United States
10 9 8 7 6 5 4 3

Abrams books are available at special discounts
when purchased in quantity for premiums
and promotions as well as fundraising or
educational use. Special editions can also be
created to specification. For details, contact
specialsales@abramsbooks.com or the
address below.

ABRAMS The Art of Books
195 Broadway, New York, NY 10007
abramsbooks.com